dusty eXile

LOOKING BACK AT
JAPANESE RELOCATION
DURING WORLD WAR II

CATHERINE EMBREE HARRIS

Mutual Publishing

Library of Congress Catalog Card
Number: 99-64887

First Printing, September 1999
Second Printing, June 2000
2 3 4 5 6 7 8 9

Design by Design Unlimited

ISBN 1-56647-274-1

Mutual Publishing
1215 Center Street, Suite 210
Honolulu, Hawaii 96816
Ph: (808) 732-1709
Fax: (808) 734-4094
e-mail: mutual@lava.net
www.mutualpublishing.com

As a nation we began by declaring that "all men are created equal." We now practically read it "all men are created equal, except Negroes." When the Know-Nothings get control, it will read "all men are created equal except Negroes and foreigners and Catholics." When it comes to this, I shall prefer emigrating to some country where they make no pretense of loving Liberty—to Russia, for instance, where despotism can be taken pure, and without the base alloy of hypocrisy.

Abraham Lincoln, letter to Joshua F. Speed, August 24, 1855

• • •

In sum, Executive Order 9066 was not justified by military necessity, and the decisions that followed from it—exclusion, detention, the ending of detention and the ending of exclusion—were not founded upon military considerations. The broad historical causes that shaped these decisions were race prejudice, war hysteria and a failure of political leadership.

Commission on Wartime Relocation and Internment of Civilians (established by Congress and signed by President Carter, 1980)

TABLE OF CONTENTS

Why *another* book about the Japanese Relocation during World War II?

Partly *because* there are still so many Americans who do not yet know the sorry tale of a single ethnic group—citizens as well as aliens—abruptly uprooted from their West Coast homes and forced to live in crowded, hastily built centers, administered by the War Relocation Authority. Military and political leaders declared the mass removal of people of Japanese ancestry to be a "military necessity." In contrast, there was no comparable evacuation of Germans or Italians, whether aliens or citizens. Only a few Germans or Italians were interned. Their families were not affected.

Also, *because* I saw the relocation from a less-than-usual point of view; I was neither a victim nor a persecutor. Many evacuees have written most eloquently and provided the most vivid accounts of the tragedy. Other books have been written by those in decision-making positions who saw justification for their actions. Administrators, lawyers, sociologists—all have had their say. I held a very lowly position on the administrative staff—not privy to reasons for government policies and not on the receiving end of those policies. The archival records have led to analytical studies from every possible point of view. I'm glad not to be such a scholar studying the documents which miss the flavor of dust in the mouth, the heat, the cold, the deep mud when it rained, the rattlesnake under the barracks steps.

And, finally, *because* the story hasn't ended. In 1998, Congress granted a $5,000 reparation to Japanese-Peruvians who were removed from Peru to an internment camp in Texas, a truly inexplicable action by the U.S. Government. Twenty thousand dollars to Japanese-Americans, aliens and citizens alike, was a token settlement; $5,000 was downright demeaning, and is being protested. Also continuing is the serious question of whether the non-awarding of the Medal of Honor to Japanese-Americans for valorous action was basically racist.

In writing my account, I have chosen to use the out-of-date terms current during World War II, even if they seem rather quaint.

The word "evacuation" was certainly a euphemism; it usually refers to short-term removal until a natural disaster or military condition can be controlled, after which the evacuees can return. A three-year incarceration hardly fits that definition.

"Internment" was applied then to camps administered by the U.S. Department of Justice for those individuals, many more than necessary, who were arrested by the FBI as possible security risks. In some cases, family members chose to join those internees. Many such internees were later released and sent to relocation centers run by the War Relocation Authority. From those centers, the "paroled" internees could receive leave clearance and move to the Midwest or the East Coast.

"Concentration" camps—whether for slave labor or extermination, as in Europe—were unknown to most of us until near the end of World War II. Some high-level government officials did indeed use the term, as records have now shown. In fact, President Roosevelt, as early as 1936, referred to the possibility of placing suspect Japanese "in a concentration camp in the event of trouble."

"Relocation" ended up having several meanings. Many Japanese-Americans were relocated first from home to an Assembly Center, then to a Relocation Center and, ultimately, were encouraged to relocate eastward to jobs, school, or the Army. A "relocation center" was nonetheless incarceration.

Whatever the terminology, it can only be hoped that this book, like many before, may help to insure that such an unwarranted violation of civil rights is not forgotten, and never repeated.

The number of people who have made this effort possible is so long that I refer you to page 133.

Far out in the Pacific Ocean over the small island of Oʻahu in the U.S. Territory of Hawaiʻi, the sun rose at 6:26 a.m. Cloudiness was forecast over the mountains, with a high in the 70s. Residents faced a usual Sunday morning—preparing breakfast, watering plants, sleeping off a hangover, changing shifts in hotels and firehouses.

An hour and a half later, the sound of planes roared overhead. No one paid much attention to such a commonplace sound. But here a child, and there a soldier looked up and recognized the "rising-sun" insignia, identifying the planes as Japanese. Bombs fell, sinking a repair ship and a minelayer, as well as battleships, destroyers, and cruisers also anchored in Pearl Harbor. Of the 126 airplanes on the ground at Wheeler Army Air Field, only 43 were left fit for service. More than 2,000 military personnel and 100 civilians were killed. It was December 7, 1941, termed by President Franklin Delano Roosevelt as "a day that will live in infamy."

The next day, 5,000 miles away in Washington, D.C., the United States declared war on Japan.

Within five months, more than 110,000 people of Japanese ancestry living in the western states of California, Oregon, Washington, and southern Arizona would be evacuated from their homes and incarcerated in makeshift Assembly Centers and, later, in ten Relocation Centers situated inland from the West Coast. Nearly 70 percent of these people were American citizens.

The reason given for this evacuation: military necessity. However, records clearly showed, even at the time, that the U.S. War Department, Military Intelligence, and the FBI saw no necessity for such a move. It was a tragic mistake that should not have happened.

Opposite page: Japanese attack on Pearl Harbor, Hawaii. (National Archives)

December 7 and Me

The announcement came
crackling over the air waves:
"We interrupt this program to bring you
a special news bulletin.
The Japanese have attacked
Pearl Harbor, Hawai'i, by air..."

On that fateful winter day, my sister and I were spending our Sunday afternoon as we usually did in Toronto—listening to the New York Philharmonic. Before we could take in the shocking news, the orchestra was back playing Shostakovich. The phone rang. My brother across town was checking to see if we'd heard the announcement. All of us had lived in Hawai'i and were familiar with the location of Pearl Harbor.

Ironically, we would join my brother for dinner that night. His wife, though born in Siberia, had grown up in Japan. She had prepared a special Japanese meal. This rare treat went underappreciated, as we continued to listen intently for further announcements on the radio.

For no particular reason, my brother, sister, and I were all temporary expatriates from the U.S., working in Toronto. My sister carried the fancy title of "Toy Adviser" in a large department store, while I toiled in another store's book section.

My older brother, John, was "professing" anthropology nearby at the University of Toronto. My brother had done his Ph.D. research in Japan in 1935–1936. The resulting book* proved to be the most "up-to-date" recording of Japanese customs and beliefs, thereby raising my brother from pedagogue to instant expert. He left Toronto within a few days for Washington, D.C., to join the Office of Strategic Services (OSS).

My sister planned to marry her "intended" before he went off to join the U.S. Navy in the summer. I toyed with the idea of volunteering as an ambulance driver. This was not a totally illogical notion, since I'd attended a Quaker college, Swarthmore, in Pennsylvania during the Spanish Civil War (1936–1939), when ambulance driving seemed the only appropriate role. Several of my college classmates had done just that, backed by emotional support from students and the reluctant blessing of the college faculty.

But, for the time being, my sister and I remained at our department store jobs.

---

*John F. Embree, *Suye Mura: A Japanese Village*, University of Chicago, 1939.

In the spring of 1942, I paid a short visit to my brother and his family in suburban Virginia, near the nation's capital. One evening, he invited his friend Al, who worked at the Office of Indian Affairs, home for dinner. When I mentioned that I would soon be looking for a job, Al insisted that I talk to his Office chief, John Collier. The name was familiar, since my father and brother knew him personally. What could I lose?

The following day, I presented myself to Mr. Collier, who, after a preliminary conversation about the family, assured me that there would be a job opening in the Indian Service. How soon could I start? September? Fine. "Just report to the Indian Service field office in Chicago."

No questions were asked about qualifications or salary. Would I get the job because my family knew the boss? Or, worse, because of an underlying attitude that anyone was qualified to work on an Indian reservation?

Whatever the reason, it didn't matter to me; I had a future.

Three months later, in August, I received a telegram from Washington asking if I'd just as soon go to a Japanese Relocation Center on Indian reservation land.

Huh? What was a relocation center? I asked myself.

While I knew nothing about Indians, I had pleasant memories of the Japanese in Hawai'i. When I was very small, a Japanese hotel waiter had "rescued" me when I floated out too far in the ocean on my water wings. A neighboring Japanese yardman often protected me from the threat of unfriendly dogs. A Japanese maid had tended to my scraped knees and stubbed toes when my mother was absent. Of course I rode to school on the trolley car with several Japanese kids all headed in the same direction.

For the first time in my life, I made a decision all on my own, based on my limited experience. I telegraphed back "yes" and started worrying whether the Japanese in a relocation center would speak English or if I could remember the limited pidgin I had learned in Honolulu. In retrospect, I find it odd that I was so uninformed.

After only a few months, my brother had parted company with the OSS and was, by August, working as a community analyst for the War

Relocation Authority in Washington. He monitored the situation in the ten relocation centers and tried to solve problems as they arose. I guess he assumed I was headed for an Indian reservation and didn't think to tell me about his new work.

I was unaware that my father had been in northern California during the initial stages of evacuation and had chanced to see families en route from home to Assembly Centers. Years later, he described a family he'd observed, each member clutching their most prized possession. The youngest, a two-year-old, carried a bundle of fresh flowers, almost more than he could hold, a sight my father never forgot.

In any case, at age 22, I faced my future. All I had to offer were the limited qualifications of a college education with an English major, and a year's work in a department store.

My real education was about to begin.

Opposite page: On a brick wall beside an air raid shelter poster, exclusion orders were posted at First and Front Streets directing removal of persons of Japanese ancestry from the first San Francisco section to be affected by evacuation. The order was issued April 1, 1942, by Lieutenant General J.L. DeWitt, and directed evacuation from this section by noon on April 7, 1942. (National Archives)

War Hysteria

On December 7, after the early morning attack on Pearl Harbor, the FBI began to round up all Japanese considered to be threats to the security of the United States—initially 367 in Hawai'i and 924 on the West Coast.

Those arrested were primarily Buddhist and Shinto priests, Japanese language teachers, publishers and editors of Japanese language papers, and businessmen with ties to Japan.

These "suspects" were taken without warning and driven away to unknown destinations. For many months, their families didn't know where the men had been taken. Leaders in Japanese communities wondered if they might also be interned without warning. Bank accounts of Japanese aliens were frozen for five days. After that time, withdrawals were limited to $100 a month.

After those individuals had been interned by the Department of Justice in camps scattered across the country, life on the surface went on as usual. Japanese school children continued to read and romp, shopkeepers served customers, and farmers sold their produce. However, the false sense of security would soon be shattered.

The American public as a whole was outraged by the attack on Pearl Harbor. Except for the War of 1812, the U.S. had never been attacked on its own soil.

President Franklin Roosevelt believed that the enemy Axis—Germany, Italy, and Japan—particularly as embodied by Adolf Hitler, represented an evil threat to democracy and human decency. However, up until Pearl Harbor, this belief was not universally shared by the American people. After World War I, the U.S. was sincerely committed to isolationism and begrudged even modest efforts to aid England with Lend-Lease and ancient destroyers.

Pearl Harbor changed all that.

Now recruiting offices overflowed with long lines of volunteers. Major industries such as shipping, railroads, steel, and automotive manufacturers retooled for war. Hollywood stars offered their services to entertain the troops and to encourage the citizenry to buy war bonds. A tobacco company even bragged, "Lucky Strike green has gone to war," and thereafter their cigarette packages were white.

In the early weeks of the war in the Pacific, grim newscasts announced that Guam had fallen, Wake Island was falling, the Philippines, Hong Kong, and Singapore were at risk.

As always, rumors made the headlines. In Hawai'i, the Japanese were accused of burning arrow shapes in the sugar cane fields to direct aircraft to Pearl Harbor and other military sites, or of blocking traffic to disrupt rescue and security efforts.

In California, there were numerous reports of spotlight signaling and ship-to-shore messages sent by shortwave radios. All such stories were carefully investigated and proved to be false, but the public was not informed of these findings.

The FBI raided the homes of Japanese people, searching for items now suspect—shortwave radios, cameras, binoculars, firearms. To aid in these searches, the FBI deputized agents who occasionally proved overzealous, if not downright destructive. The FBI reports admitted, but did not publicize, that they had found no illegal radio transmitters, or anything else dangerous or unexplainable. However, as the weeks passed, the FBI made more arrests, including many of Japanese people whose only fault lay in being recognized as "community leaders."

Of the 5,000 Japanese-Americans in military uniform, virtually all were released from active service and relegated to K.P. or yard duty. All other *nisei* (second generation) were classified as 4C—aliens not subject to military service.

In 1941, some 125,000 people of Japanese ancestry lived in the 48 states. Of these, 112,000 lived in Washington, Oregon, and California. About 93 percent resided in California, where they comprised barely one percent of the state's population. The *issei* (first generation) aliens, average age 60, had come to America before 1924. That year the Immigration Act was passed, excluding "all aliens ineligible to citizenship," limiting naturalization to "free white persons and to aliens of African nativity and to persons of African descent." No Asians could look forward to U.S. citizenship.

Many of the Japanese *issei* had lived in the U.S. for more than 40 years. Their *nisei* children—two-thirds of the Japanese population—were American citizens. They were concerned about their parents, but did not believe that they themselves could be declared "enemies."

As war hysteria and racist editorials dominated most newspapers, the *issei* became seriously alarmed. They burned photos and letters from relatives in Japan, sold or buried treasured antique *samurai* swords and all evidence of their traditional Japanese culture, even destroying their children's Girl's Day dolls and Boy's Day paper carp. This protective reaction must have had a wrenching effect on an ethnic group that prided itself on its heritage. Cherished mementos, memories of birthdays and festivals—all gone.

Too many people succumbed to racial hysteria. Landlords broke rental leases, utility companies demanded instant cash payments, or threatened to cut off services. Merchants put signs in their windows: "No Japs allowed." Caucasian customers turned their backs on Japanese florists and grocery stores. Milk companies and grocers refused to "trade with the enemy." Truckers and wholesalers no longer accepted goods from Japanese farms and nurseries. Japanese produce merchants could not renew their licenses nor get permits to collect sales taxes, so they were forced out of business. State and county employees were fired. School children lost their Caucasian friends. Teachers faltered in their teaching so that the students learned more about discrimination than about equality.

Some Japanese families received threatening phone calls. Others noticed increased car traffic on their quiet residential streets—some racing, some honking, some just cruising by. Here and there shops and farm buildings were set afire. Police and fire departments seemed uninterested and offered no leadership to stop such activities. Violent personal attacks, officially recorded, numbered fewer than 50. But the reports flashed up and down the West Coast. Anxiety turned to outright alarm.

Pressure mounted. Ordinary citizens, fed on false rumors and honest fears, panicked. Others, more self-serving, recognized an opportunity to drive out the Japanese. Envious farmers who coveted Japanese land pressured the local farmers' Grange organization to press for evacuation. Even though the Japanese on farms or in small shops were not competing for union jobs, American Federation of Labor leaders spoke up loudly for jobs for "real Americans." The prejudiced claimed to seek Aryan purity. The media—partly radio but mainly the newspapers—fanned the flames of fear and bigotry.

Political leaders and the military responded with new regulations, such as an 8 p.m. to 6 a.m. curfew. No Japanese, whether alien or citizen, could travel more than five miles from home. Such regulations prevented many students from attending school and many parents from earning a living.

Events moved so fast that those opposed to evacuation were unable to slow the process. Barely three months after Pearl Harbor, on February 19, 1942, President Franklin Roosevelt signed Executive Order 9066. This order gave the Secretary of War authority to designate "military areas" and to exclude "any and all persons" from those areas. The wording was deliberately vague to avoid legal and constitutional questions that might arise if exclusion were limited to the Japanese.

Just two days after the President signed Executive Order 9066, a Congressional committee, headed by Representative John Tolan of California, opened hearings in San Francisco, to be followed by hearings in Portland and Seattle. This House Committee was set up to "inquire further into the interstate migration of citizens" and consider "the problems of evacuation of enemy aliens and others from prohibited military zones."

The FBI and the Department of War had declared that evacuation was not necessary. Church groups, particularly but not exclusively Quakers, testified against evacuation, as did university presidents and faculty, and many concerned citizens.

The only organization of American-born *nisei* in existence was the Japanese American Citizens League (JACL), composed of a few young people in several chapters on the West Coast. The League began in 1930, but had served largely as a social organization. While the *nisei* did register to vote, they were reluctant to engage in political affairs. In 1936, the JACL adopted noble goals that urged the *nisei* to become good Americans through civic participation. In the face of general hostility, these goals remained abstract and unachievable. The League had neither the experience nor the political clout to protest discrimination effectively.

In early 1942, the JACL chapters accepted contributions and distributed money and goods to the needy families whose funds had been frozen, who had lost jobs, or were denied licenses to carry on their businesses. Since most of the Japanese newspapers had been closed

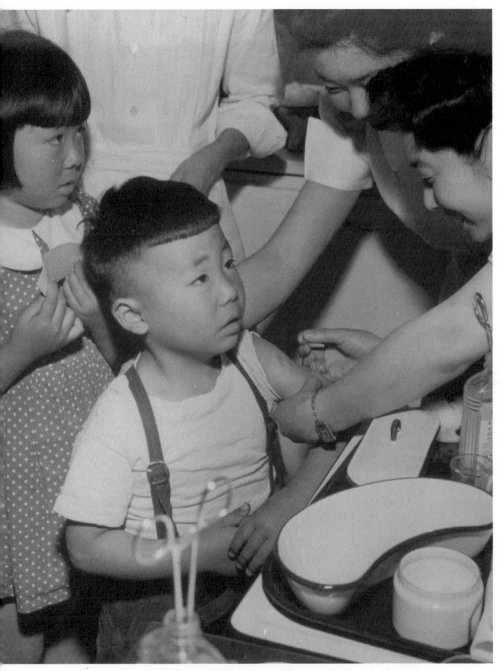

Opposite page top: The father of this small family is attending to their luggage and bed rolls. They will spend the duration in a War Relocation Authority center. Opposite page inset: Two children of the Mochida family await the evacuation bus. Above: Evacuees in Assembly Centers are vaccinated by fellow evacuees. (National Archives)

down, JACL chapters collected and mimeographed what information they could get from federal officials, and distributed such news from door to door. What little influence the JACL had was used to urge alien *issei* and citizen *nisei* to cooperate with government orders. To demonstrate loyalty, the JACL continued to press for the right of the *nisei* to serve in the military, yet the Selective Service classified the *nisei* as 4C—enemy aliens.

On March 1, less than one month into the Congressional hearings, Lt. General John DeWitt, commander of the Western Defense Command, issued Proclamation No. 1, designating the western half of California, Oregon, and Washington, as well as the southern third of Arizona, as military areas. On March 11, the Wartime Civil Control Administration was established, with Colonel Karl Bendetsen as director, to carry out the evacuation of all persons of Japanese ancestry.

The Western Defense Command pushed the restricted military zones further inland to cover virtually all the areas where the Japanese-Americans lived and worked. Notices of Public Law 77-503 were posted on utility poles, in post offices, and city halls—INSTRUCTIONS TO ALL PERSONS OF JAPANESE ANCESTRY—telling people where and when to report for evacuation. Hope died.

People on Terminal Island in California and Bainbridge Island in Washington had just 48 hours to leave. Those on the coast were allowed two weeks. A lifetime of possessions and necessities, such as clothing, medicine, keepsakes, had to fit into what each person could carry, usually two suitcases or boxes.

The panic sales began. Farms, equipment, houses, cars, furniture, appliances, clothing, pianos, sewing machines, record players—such possessions had to be sold immediately. Some buyers offered ludicrously low prices or threatened to tell the FBI if the sellers didn't accept the offers. People in some rural communities returned the last day to grab anything that remained unsold. Many *issei* were wiped out financially.

The Farm Security Administration was supposed to insure a fair deal on crops and real estate. The Federal Reserve Bank was supposed to safeguard evacuees' other properties. It didn't happen. Belatedly, the U.S. Government offered storage facilities, but with no insurance protection.

In the midst of the stress and avidity, many non-Japanese neighbors proved to be caring, honest, and helpful. When evacuation became a reality, such neighbors and other friends paid fair prices, offered free storage, and kept in touch with the evacuees. They reported on property, sent packages, and provided a slim thread of hope for the future. A *nisei* woman shook her head in wonderment and said, "Our worst enemies are Californians, but so are our best friends."

The evacuees were told nothing about destination, climate, or duration, so no one knew what to pack. Where were they going? To prison? Would they remain there, wherever, until the war ended? Would they be shipped to Japan? Did the number assigned to each family mean they could stay together? If a father had been interned, would he rejoin the family? Some families still didn't know where the father had been interned. Any censored letters told little.

Young children cried without understanding why they had to leave friends, pets, and familiar surroundings. Older children stood by silently, not entirely realizing that their childhood was now behind them.

Those living in Washington, Oregon, and northern California went to Assembly Centers at race tracks and fair grounds, established in just 28 days. Conditions there ranged from very bad to worse. Guard towers with bright search lights were in place. The legacy of Santa Anita and Tanforan survives in bitter stories and wry cartoons. Evacuees recall the overpowering smell of horses in the stables, inadequate plumbing for too many people crowded in too small an area. People shared sleeping space with rats, mice, spiders, and, of course, horseflies. Many suffered respiratory allergies.

Everyone stood in long lines for everything—meals, mail, a laundry tub, the canteen, the bathroom, you name it. Hot water was rarely available. In the common lavatories, antiseptic footbaths were designed to prevent infections, but the heavily-chlorinated solution was more likely to burn the skin off than sanitize.

People used to eating healthy fruits, vegetables, and rice now faced unappealing Army food; canned hash and pork and beans were the daily fare. When the food spoiled, people got sick. Diners were required to bring their own plate and utensils, which they rinsed in a common container of cold and greasy water. The young people craved more food, particularly ice cream and sweets of any kind. Caucasian friends, when they could locate individual evacuees, brought food and necessities not furnished by the military. Visiting space was limited, so friends spent more time waiting outside than visiting inside. All packages, of course, had to be inspected.

Assembly Centers were pits of misery for several dreadful months. The War Relocation Authority was not yet in full operation. The military was in charge. Curfew began at 8 p.m. Heads were counted twice a day. Any activities to relieve boredom were initiated by the "inmates" and included such pastimes as a ball team, a nursery school, a reading group, a victory garden, and English classes.

At the relocation camps established later, the Assembly Center "graduates" settled down more quickly, fixed up barracks faster, and began activities sooner than the evacuees who'd gone from home directly

to relocation camps. Those from Assembly Centers had been through the worst; the relocation camps offered a bit more space and didn't smell so much.

In the two earliest relocation camps—Manzanar in California and Poston in Arizona—the evacuees arrived directly from their homes. These camps were not as grim as the Assembly Centers, but the evacuees took longer than the "grads" to settle in. The difference may have resulted from the fact that the Assembly Centers were in familiar territory, whereas Manzanar and Poston were located in distant, desolate places far from home.

Thus began three years of life in "relocation" camps.

• • •

A *tanka* composed in an Assembly Center:

Plate in hand,
I stand in line,
Losing my resolve
To hide my tears.

I see my mother
In the aged woman
who comes
And I yield to her
My place in line.

Four months have passed,
And at last I learn
To call this horse stall
My family's home.*

*Yoshiko Uchida, *Desert Exile: The Uprooting of a Japanese American Family*, Bancroft Library, University of California Berkeley. Written by Yukari, the pen name of the author's mother.

Opposite page: Lunch time cafeteria style, where many thousands of evacuees of Japanese ancestry are temporarily housed pending transfer to War Relocation Authority centers where they will spend the duration. (National Archives)

Westward Ho!

By August 1942, while the evacuees
were coming to grips with their bleak new
environment and working to make it habitable,
I had yet to begin.

In Chicago, I presented myself at the regional headquarters of the Office of Indian Affairs, which did business in a drab downtown building darkened by sooty windows. No one had told me what I might do among either the Indians or the Japanese. An indifferent civil servant asked me what job I was applying for. I'd been wondering about that myself.

He solved the problem by handing me a list of possible jobs—a grubby, double-sided sheet, six columns wide in very fine print. What could I do, with a Bachelor of Arts degree, a major in English and minors in French and Fine Arts? My entire employment history had been ten months working in a book department.

I was truly daunted, but a fast glance through the letter "A" provided an answer to our mutual satisfaction—Assistant Teacher—with the munificent salary of $1,200 per year. Indeed a step up from $15 a week.

The man handed me a Form 57 to fill out. With such a short employment history, I filled it out quickly. He informed me that I was destined to work at the Colorado River Relocation Center, commonly referred to as Poston. Where was that? Back of beyond, on Indian land outside the town of Parker, Arizona, hardly findable on any map.

I told the civil servant that I could leave in three days. Excited to start a new job and a new career, I boarded the train to chug west into my future.

The three-day trip seemed short. I watched first the prairies and then the mountains go by. The Santa Fe train pulled into Phoenix in the morning, giving me a whole day before a connecting train would carry me to my destination. I was charmed by Phoenix, which reminded me of Honolulu in the 1930s—low buildings, stucco or adobe in pale colors, palm trees in unexpected places. I bought a splendid seersucker dress at Goldwater's Department Store and sampled hot chili for the first time. Everywhere I went, the friendly, drawling Arizonans wished me well and urged me to "Hurry back." I made an instant vow that if the Relocation

Opposite page: Evacuees of Japanese ancestry fish for carp in the canal on the northwest side of this War Relocation center. The boys caught eight fish on bent pins with bread as bait. (National Archives)

Center job didn't work out, I'd return to Phoenix and be a salesclerk or a waitress. I didn't want to leave Arizona.

The dusty, all-coach train to Parker pulled out of Phoenix at 6 p.m. and arrived at Parker four hours later. Parker is west and a bit north of Phoenix, below the Parker Dam and across the Colorado River from Earp, California, named for the famed Marshal Wyatt Earp of a hundred Hollywood westerns.

I was the only passenger to alight from the train before it continued further west to California. No brass band, no one at all to greet me upon my arrival. As was usually the case in a small town on a rail line, the two-story hotel stood across the road from the small train

Above: View of main street in Parker. Near this desert town, the War Relocation Authority will maintain a center for evacuees of Japanese ancestry on the Colorado River Indian reservation. (National Archives)

station. With no street lights, I could see only the rooftop sign: Grand View Hotel. I picked up my belongings and crossed the road. The shabby hotel lobby was deserted. On the counter to the right sat the usual round bell to ring for attention. I did, and an unfriendly looking man slouched out from a back room. I asked politely for a single room for the night. "No rooms," he replied curtly.

Later I learned that the hotel was never full, so I could only assume that women were the unwelcome "guests." I explained that I was headed for the Colorado River Japanese Relocation Center. He shrugged. I looked over at the spring-sprung chairs and announced that I'd have to sit it out, right there, until morning. He snapped to attention. "Oh, no!" he protested. "Call the Indian Service." Reaching under the counter, he brought forth a telephone and a limp sheet of phone numbers.

By now, it was nearly 11 p.m. It seemed a rude hour to summon up a government bureaucrat, but I had no choice. The bureaucrat responded nobly and with dispatch. A car soon appeared and drove me to Indian Service headquarters, where I was shown to a narrow, immaculately clean room with a bed, a dresser, and one chair. I was told where and when to report for breakfast.

The sun and I were up early and had a companionable time while I shortened my new dress to make a stylish appearance on my first day. By 8 a.m., the temperature had risen above 100 degrees. A slight, dapper man, Bill Barrett, a maintenance supervisor of some kind, appeared in a jeep.

He drove me south to the Relocation Center in Poston. During the ride, Mr. Barrett identified the flora—the mesquite that was like the *kiawe* in Hawai'i, the puffy tumbleweed blown along by the wind, sparse shrubs the same color as the desert. Cactus, tall and short, grew everywhere, and spiky arroweed, but no such thing as a shade tree. Birds were not much in evidence, but Mr. Barrett alerted me to the swift passage of roadrunners as they sped across the road, preferring running to flying.

In all directions, near or far, rose flat-topped mesas, the same noncolor as the whole terrain. Over time I learned to note the subtle changes. In the early morning, the rising sun tinted the outlines of the eastern mesas in gold, then sent piercing rays to streak the western ones until the heavens were awash with brilliant light. The sky was wide and limpid. The evening sky changed from brown to pale blue to violet, and back to deep purple and into darkness. Gradual alterations, undramatic, but beautiful.

Seasonal changes in the desert do not compare to the flamboyance of eastern flowers and autumn leaves, but the cactus which blooms modestly into yellow or pink or lavender gladdens those who pause to notice. That first September morning, the landscape appeared to be all one color.

About halfway along the 17-mile route, my escort pointed ahead to a massive dust cloud hanging low. "That's Poston," he said. I soon discovered that dust was the never-ending reality of camp life. Poston was located on the silt of what had been Colorado River bottom land, as fine as talcum powder, pervasive, and wonderfully fertile when encouraged with a little water.

Bill Barrett slowed as we approached a sign warning civilians away. Shortly we reached a gate and small sentry box manned by Military Police. A couple of young, bored soldiers in uniform went through the motions of checking us in. They knew the jeep and the driver and, since I was obviously not Japanese, they waved us through.

And here was Poston! Also known as Toaston, Roaston, and Duston. Row after row of black tar-papered barracks stretched over the colorless bare land toward the horizon. The population of some 17,000 evacuees made it the third largest city in Arizona after Phoenix and Tucson. Here in Camp I, nearly 10,000 individuals and families had been living for three months. Three miles down the road, Camp II had nearly 5,000 people and, three miles further, Camp III had slightly more than 3,000.

I didn't have any idea of what a Relocation Center would look like, but I surely wasn't prepared for the bleakness. As I grew accustomed to it, I forgot how the Center looked, even how hot it was. Yet I never forgot the dust; no one could, since we walked through it and lived in it day after day. The occasional dust storm could even be frightening. Not only did the infernal stuff dirty the clothes and powder the hair, it could darken the sky and fog the vision. Neighboring buildings disappeared, and even indoors the air was misty and polluted. Children were frightened and often lost in the bewildering veil around them. But this "experience" lay in my future.

On the left, as we drove in, a few white-washed administrative buildings stood in contrast to the black tar-paper barracks across the road. Mr. Barrett stopped at the door of the central building to let me off. With a friendly wave, he drove away.

I had arrived!

Within minutes, I met Fran, my roommate for the first year. She was both the Assistant Principal and Counselor of the Camp I High School. She stood tall, prematurely gray, moving too fast to be stately, but was still an impressive figure. Her warmth and friendliness quickly made me feel like part of the orderly chaos that prevailed.

Fran escorted me across the road to our tar-papered barracks, no different from the rest of camp, except that we had proper beds, dressers, chairs, and some sort of floor covering. Also, the administrative barracks each had its own latrine, instead of a communal one serving a whole block. Modesty was not well served for the evacuees or administrative personnel. Our toilets were doorless, but partitioned, cubbyholes. The evacuees had no partitions, so the women improvised with corrugated cardboard sides from packing cases which, unfortunately, disintegrated rapidly. All the showers were large, open squares, which could serve four at a time. Claire, a librarian in our barracks, could not face showering in public and, at first, waited until midnight to bathe. What with temperatures often reaching 120 degrees and the ever-present dust, frequent showering was essential, no matter the arrangements. For the older evacuees, a shower was no substitute for the deep-heated satisfaction of a proper *furo*. At least Poston suffered no water shortage, with the wide Colorado River nearby.

The evacuee women who worked in the administrative buildings put us to shame. They showered and changed clothes at noon and again before supper. To be always fresh and clean with the few clothes they had, they spent their evenings and early mornings handwashing and ironing endless rounds of laundry. We were much less meticulous, but we did brush up on our own laundry skills.

Any new arrival who couldn't document a recent typhoid shot received a double dose from the staff doctor. There were a lot of very sick people those first weeks. When diarrhea attacked the evacuees, as it often did, chamber pots or reasonable facsimiles became the norm for everyone, not just the very young and very old. Also, the plumbing tended to break down in the early months to add to the misery.

Fran and I slept too soundly to be disturbed by the traffic across the hall. Officially we were supposed to work 48 hours a week, but no one did. Administrative personnel were always in motion. Evenings we wrote reports, or attended meetings all over camp—usually in the mess halls—about school shortages, opportunities for relocation, camp problems, and block manager's suggestions. Later there were PTA meetings and teacher's conferences to attend and dances to chaperone or youth groups to supervise.

In general, all of the women went barelegged, but a few administration sticklers insisted that their evacuee secretaries wear stockings—cruel and unusual punishment in the desert heat—and expensive, if obtainable at all during those war-shortage days. The staff men wore long-sleeved shirts, even jackets, on formal occasions such as meetings with the Poston Council or the PTA. Their slacks were long. No one, male or female, considered wearing shorts.

Opposite page: Landscaping done by evacuee residents of Camp Number I. (National Archives)

The Middle of Nowhere

The War Relocation Authority,
under pressure of time to house 110,000 people,
settled for whatever locations were available.

They found ten sites under federal jurisdiction. The two in Arizona were on Indian reservation land. The others—two in California, plus one each in Utah, Colorado, Idaho, and Wyoming, and two in Arkansas—were placed where Civilian Conservation Corps or National Youth Administration camps had been just a few years before, now abandoned. All were isolated and on undeveloped land. The WRA camps were laid out to army specifications, suitable for healthy young men in rugged military training, not for families with infants, and especially not for the elderly and the sick.

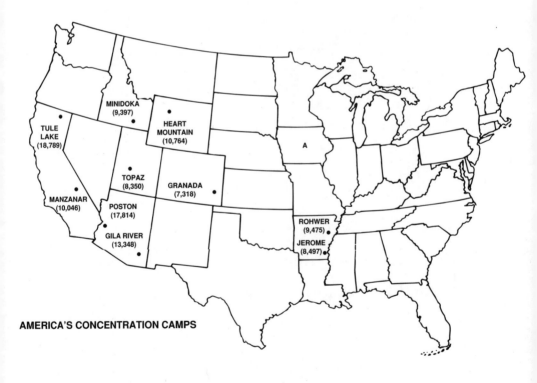

AMERICA'S CONCENTRATION CAMPS

Above: John Tateishi *And Justice For All*: An oral history of the Japanese-American Detention Camps, Random House, Inc., 1984.

The bulldozers came and chewed up the landscape. No living plant remained, only dust or sand, depending on the location of the camp. Some centers were colder, such as Heart Mountain, Wyoming, and Tule Lake, California. Some were hotter, like Poston and Gila River, in Arizona. Manzanar, in California, had high mountains; Poston had mesas. Jerome, Arkansas, had the Mississippi River; Poston had the Colorado River. All of them had dust. The Army erected single-wall barracks quickly and cheaply, constructed with the poorest grade of green, knot-holed lumber. The floor boards were loose; dust blew in, covering everything. Even when can lids covered the holes and mats covered the floors, the dust persisted. Occasional breezes blew puffs of dust in, even around the nail holes. The starkness of the landscape of tar-papered barracks seemed to stretch almost to the horizon.

Most of the evacuees arrived at the Centers in crowded, hot trains. The railroad cars were old and dirty. All the way through California, the window curtains were pulled down in the daytime, decreasing the flow of air. A needless precaution, since few of these people had ever been a hundred miles from home; the passing scenery conveyed nothing. Military troop trains had priority, so the evacuee trains waited on sidings longer than they were in transit. The trip could take 24 hours to Poston in western Arizona, or five long days to Arkansas. For food, the evacuees depended on what they had brought with them; no provision was made for infants or the sick.

The travelers sat quietly on the hot plush seats, too stunned to protest. For all these people, the world had been turned upside down. Parents without answers felt helpless to explain this devastating uprooting. The children could not find anything in the Declaration of Independence or the Constitution to make sense of their present reality.

Young couples with small, crying toddlers had little strength to give comfort; they could find none for themselves. Babies were sick and without medicine. A few teenage boys who'd attended a last movie a few days earlier had caught and were now abloom with measles. Older teenagers were bitter, sullen. For them, it was a bleak spring—the baseball players missed the season, high school seniors didn't graduate.

Thus, in May 1942, the first evacuees reached Poston. After debarking from the train in the little town of Parker in the late afternoon, they faced a 17-mile truck ride to the camp. It was dark by the time they received their block and barracks assignments and were trucked to what would be "home" for no one knew how long.

As each evacuee arrived, he or she received a coarse bag with instructions to fill it with straw from a nearby bale. Each person had a cot and two army blankets. For light, a single electric bulb on a cord hung from the roof. The barracks had no running water. Mothers washed their babies in laundry tubs, hoping there would be some hot water. There were not nearly enough laundry tubs for the number of inhabitants to do their family laundry in the ever-dusty environment.

The camp was divided into blocks, each consisting of two rows of eight barracks, housing 250 to 300 people. Between the two rows of barracks stood latrines and laundry buildings. Four blocks grouped together were separated from others by wide firebreaks to prevent the spread of fire. In each block, one barracks was designated as the mess hall and another the recreation hall.

Each residential barracks was divided into four apartments, 20 by 25 feet—habitation for families of up to eight people. For smaller groups, the units measured 20 by 16 feet. Single men lived in open dormitory space. Eventually each unit had a heating stove, but early on, only a hole in the roof offered the promise of future warmth; now it served only as another entry for wind and dust.

The mess halls offered communal dining at tables with benches attached—a severe challenge to grace and modesty. Even the most proper and formal *issei* ladies soon took to wearing slacks. Before long, families gave up eating together, since the children preferred eating with their friends.

The food allowance for evacuees was less than 45 cents a day. Rice was scarce and, early on, the menu of Vienna sausage and sauerkraut did not fit with the hot climate. Cheese and apple butter, not favorite dietary items, were in ample supply. At first, the mess hall workers were evacuee volunteers or those arbitrarily assigned to the work. Later, cooks with restaurant experience took over the mess halls and the Army adjusted their supplies to suit the population. A really good chef could

Above: Unloading beds for evacuees. Inset: Evacuees of Japanese ancestry are filling straw ticks for mattresses. (National Archives)

achieve great popularity and sometimes wielded considerable influence by catering to favored friends.

In most Relocation Centers, including Poston Camps II and III, the school classes were grouped in a single block. In Poston I, recreation halls throughout the camps were commandeered for classroom purposes, each building divided into three sections. For high school students, the "campus" was immense. The mess halls in each block became, by default, the recreation buildings.

Each block had a block manager to tend to everyday demands— maintaining grounds and buildings, distributing information from the Administration, mediating arguments among block residents.

The winds of prejudice had swept up a whole ethnic group, removing them from their homes, communities, occupations, and dropping them into ten bleak camps. From farms and cities had come gardeners, fishermen, artists, hotel keepers, importers, barbers, and shoemakers—strangers crowded together indiscriminately. In any block, the residents shared only their Japanese heritage and the "look" of the enemy.

Opposite page: Living quarters of evacuees of Japanese ancestry at this War Relocation Authority center as seen from the water tower. (National Archives)

Instant Immersion

I had arrived in Poston on a Saturday.
On Monday morning, I was trucked off to an
Indian school for the closing meetings
of a teacher-training seminar.

This two-week session was intended for the evacuees who'd been recruited to offset the expected severe shortage of appointed teachers from outside the camp. Five teachers from California and seven from the Indian Service constituted the faculty. Twenty-two evacuee kids were rounded up for practice-teaching purposes. Most of the evacuee teachers-to-be were my contemporaries, all in our twenties. The majority had had two or three years of college, a few had had four. As the first official teacher to arrive from the outside, I was the only Caucasian trainee.

Since the training session was winding down, I was too late to benefit from the classes or to receive my very own teaching syllabus, prepared by a task force at Stanford University. I doubt that the syllabus would have made much difference anyway, due to my unpreparedness in subject matter, lack of teaching experience, and absence of confidence. Fortunately, I had the chance to meet some of my colleagues who seemed undaunted by the prospect of teaching.

I didn't have much time to get to know my fellow teachers. There was George, probably in his late thirties, a *kibei*, the term used for one born in the U.S. but educated extensively in Japan. George spoke fluent Japanese, but would be teaching Spanish. He was six feet tall, unusual for a Japanese in those days. With his wispy beard and placid manner, he seemed to have stepped out of an ancient scroll painting of a contemplative poet.

Hajime, young and broad-shouldered with shining black hair, needed only a woven straw helmet and broad sword at his waist to personify a stalwart *samurai*.

Anne and her husband, who worked in the Employment Office, were among the few articulate activists with strong union convictions established well before evacuation. I never knew her well enough to understand her union sympathies, since the American Federation of Labor in California was adamantly opposed to all Japanese, and had testified in favor of the mass evacuation.

Ben's father and uncle had farmed in Riverside and had been spirited off to Lordsburg, New Mexico, for no reason other than being community leaders. Ben's mother and her three sons and three daughters were among the early arrivals in Poston. Her first order of business was to hang a blanket in the middle of the "apartment" to separate the boys from the girls. Ben already had vision problems which would eventually lead to total blindness. He plowed right into the teaching of all forms of high school math. Others, like Tad and Sunao and Marvel, all calmly accepted their unexpected designation as teachers.

As a total stranger in a group that had come to know each other, I was an eavesdropper, rather than a participant in conversations. Bob had a younger sister afflicted with polio who had difficulty walking in the deep dust. Sumi, a worrier, spoke about her mother's intractable diarrhea. And Jake bragged about the two apple boxes he'd "found" in the back of the mess hall which he'd converted into a desk at the end of his cot. Setsuko reported that her father, although still silent, was collecting mesquite wood and creating name signs for the doors in his block. Shig laughed about his kid brother catching a three-inch fish in the irrigation canal fed by the Colorado River and demanding that the fish be cooked for supper.

Even though I'd joined the training session late, I shared in the closing ceremonies, listening attentively to the final high-minded summary-principles, philosophy, and sincere exhortations to go forth and educate the uprooted children.

The last half-day of the session was a delight. The Indian school staff provided the refreshments and the evacuee trainees put on the entertainment. Ken, I remember most vividly. He was slightly built and a dapper dude who, with his ukulele, sang "I've Got Spurs That Jingle, Jangle, Jingle"—my first "western" song, which surely owed more to Tin Pan Alley than to the Santa Fe Trail.

We broke up in a state of euphoria, prepared to march out and give the kids the best damn education they'd ever had.

During the weeks between our training and the opening of school, I had a chance to look beyond the wide firebreak dividing the Administration from the rest of the camp and to meet more of my future colleagues on both sides of that break.

Every night for several weeks, I met the train to greet the new teachers who continued to arrive from the outside. Texan Slim Jim, who

POSTON UNIT I

x Sewage Lagoon

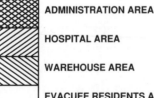

ADMINISTRATION AREA

HOSPITAL AREA

WAREHOUSE AREA

EVACUEE RESIDENTS AREA
(ENCLOSED NUMBER INDICATES NUMBER OF BLOCK)

Above: Poston Unit I (From Alexander H. Leighton, *The Governing of Men: General Principles and Recommendations Based on Experience at a Japanese Relocation Camp.* Copyright 1945. Reprinted by permission of Princeton University Press)

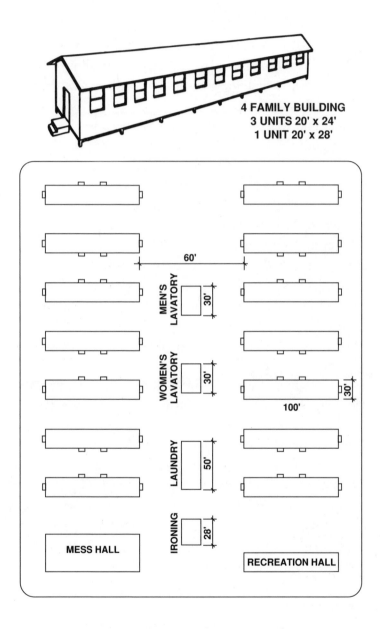

Above: The plan of a typical block at Poston. (From Edward Spicer et al., *Impounded People: Japanese-Americans in the Relocation Centers.* Copyright © 1969 The Arizona Board of Regents. Reprinted by permission of the University of Arizona Press.)

drove the old army truck, never talked much. He was missing several front teeth, so his drawling remarks included some whistling. He always picked me up on time for the train, prepared for whatever came—late train, no teachers on board, or a teacher debarking all upset by the heat or the lateness or the first look at the Poston barracks. His laid-back attitude had a calming effect.

The administrative buildings and barracks were air-conditioned by water dripping through excelsior panels over the inside fans. These contraptions raised the humidity inside and left puddles outside. Some of the evacuees solved the heat problem by excavating under the barracks to provide a cool, shady spot. At least one such "cellar" was raided by security police in the belief that the "owner" was making moonshine.

My roommate Fran was responsible for the time-consuming job of obtaining transcripts from the schools the students had come from. Some transcripts never came, so some kids were placed in the wrong grades at the beginning. Complicating the difficulty of obtaining transcripts was the matter of student names. Evacuee students were listed in camp by their given Japanese names, while on the West Coast most of them had gone by "western" names.

Wherever Fran went, I tagged along. Thus, I saw the evacuee blocks close up and marveled at what had been done to lessen the desolation. Friends on the outside sent in packets of seed, so flowers bloomed by the wooden steps. Castor beans grew against the barracks walls—hardy, but poisonous, so harried mothers were forever scolding and grabbing toddlers away from the tempting beans. Cactus and wild grasses transplanted from the desert relieved the blackness of the tar paper. The Colorado River silt on which Poston was built needed only water to produce. Official and unofficial irrigation made the desert bloom profusely. But a few feet away from the barracks, we all walked through the powdery dust. When it rained, walking through the deep mud was even more unpleasant.

Inside the barracks, clever people found practical ways to fight the dust battle. Kids dug for nails around the construction debris and scavenged can lids from the mess hall. They covered the knotholes with can lids to keep out the dust or light from the next "apartment." This also muted, a little, the voices of anger and anguish and the crying of babies. Sadi and Bob received nails as a wedding present, so they put up a partition for privacy.

The military builders left behind piles of scrap lumber and nails and other useful items that were forbidden to the evacuees. The Administration was sensible enough to ignore such rules and looked the other way. Evacuees used that scrap to build an astonishing amount of furniture such as bookcases, dressers, and shelving. Some were crude, but others were beautifully crafted.

The women found ways to cover and curtain the windows. Families with money in reserve ordered other refinements from the catalogs in the cooperative community store. People could make their quarters prettier, but they couldn't make the space any bigger or more private.

Among the fellow teachers was Kats, who had been drafted into the teacher-training session with less than two years of college behind him. He taught math with little confidence and no books. After a day of teaching, he returned "home" each day to his bitterly and loudly abusive *issei* father, his silent mother, and a young sister who suffered severe asthma attacks whenever the wind gusted up the dust. In this cramped environment, Kats planned assignments for the morrow while sitting on the end of his cot at a small table.

Kazu, a 19-year-old girl, had been tops in all her high school commercial courses in California. She felt lucky to have a clerical job in the air-conditioned welfare office. Her brother, a *kibei*, had returned to the U.S. two months before Pearl Harbor after spending two years in Japan. At 13, he was a sullen boy who extolled the superiority of life in Japan. Their father had been the principal of a language school in Los Angeles, which proved sufficient cause to send him to the Lordsburg, New Mexico, internment camp, leaving behind a frightened wife to cope with evacuation. The family shared their apartment with Kazu's maternal uncle, who wandered the desert during the day and played *go* with other single men in the mess hall in the evening. Kazu usually spent her evenings in the laundry building, washing and ironing her cotton dresses. There, she found friendship among other girls doing the same thing.

Elderly Mr. Sato lived quietly with a thin, makeshift curtain between his bed and the beds of three bachelor *issei* brothers. The apartment was furnished with the bare necessities—two tables, some shelves, and hooks nailed into the studs. They had no chairs, so all sat on their cots. Mr. Sato regularly visited the welfare office to ask if his wife could be transferred to Poston from a mental hospital in California. The answer was always no; Poston was not equipped to treat her schizophrenic condition.

Within a very short time, we in the Administration established friendships with people of similar attitudes. There were those who wanted to be there, who, in some way, wanted to make up for a terrible injustice. At the other extreme were those who despised the Japanese and held the job for the steady pay. In between were the professionals, who did what needed doing, and did it competently. Many of this middle group were people with skills who'd previously served on Indian reservations. Our in-house Community Analyst dubbed our two extreme groups "people-minded" and "stereotype-minded," and so we were.

There was a persistent problem of terminology—what to call "us" and what to call "them." At first we were termed "whites," which was soon changed to "Caucasian." The War Relocation Authority declared us "appointed personnel"—too much of a mouthful, so it was shortened to APs, commonly pronounced "apes" by the evacuees, although they usually referred to us as *hakujin* (white person). We called ourselves "staff."

For the 110,000 Japanese, no term was satisfactory. Deplorably, some of the APs never gave up saying "Japs." Differentiating the alien *issei* from the younger citizen *nisei* or *kibei* (if they were citizens who'd been educated in Japan) was just too cumbersome. "Colonists" didn't take, nor did "settlers." "Relocatees" was awkward. "Internees" was a term reserved for those in the Justice Department internment camps. Most of us settled for "evacuees."

Personal visitors were rare. My mother would not come closer than Phoenix, but my father made the effort. I gave him an uncensored tour of the camp and introduced him to assorted colleagues and to the masterful martinis served at the Corral in Parker. My brother, now a

Community Analyst in the Washington office of the WRA, sent word of his imminent arrival. At the same time, Norris, the Reports Officer, was expecting an unnamed Washington official on the same train. We waited together at the depot. I suspected that my brother was that "official." Norris was certain that the brother of such a lowly employee could not be an "important personage." I was right—ha ha—which gave me considerable satisfaction.

After a few months, I'd changed from casual employee to impassioned crusader. I was outraged at the unconstitutionality of uprooting citizens and their law-abiding parents and sending them into unhappy exile. I was indignant with President Roosevelt for following biased advice about danger from the Japanese. I hated the stupidity of the military mind and the Californians whose historic prejudice had precipitated this upheaval. I was even mad at my Midwest friends and relatives who were as ignorant as I had been while all this was taking place.

Well, they weren't allowed to stay ignorant very long! As early as October 1942, some evacuees had received permission to attend college in the Middle West or on the East Coast. My parents in Chicago were often the first stop for relocating *nisei* on the overland railroad. My parents, singly or together, met trains, figured out connections to obscure towns and colleges, provided bed and board and bath, and even tender loving care to these first young and scared advance guard venturing into unknown territory. These young people disarmed their adversaries with their modesty, gratitude, and dedication to be better than the best.

Of course, my parents were not alone in their efforts to open up jobs and acceptance in Chicago. But not all the other enlightened do-gooders had an infuriated daughter to answer to.

Stresses
and Strains

The War Relocation Authority faced a multitude
of problems. As a new federal organization,
it undertook a complex assignment: to remove
more than 100,000 people from the West Coast
and place them in ten new locations, and then
"govern" them for an indefinite period.

That was the first meaning of "relocation." Later the word would mean the movement of people out of centers back into community life for employment and schooling.

The first step was to find locations and build quarters as rapidly as possible. Once the centers were built, the WRA had to transport the people from temporary Assembly Centers. The WRA had to provide all the services necessary for a community at each of the ten sites, including housing and food. Not surprisingly in a country gearing up for total war, the WRA's needs received low priority. Shortages of essential supplies such as lumber and plumbing pipes, even nails, delayed construction.

A staff had to be hired—administrators, engineers, teachers, medical personnel, police and firemen, agricultural supervisors, ad infinitum. Dillon Myers, the national Director, came from the U.S. Department of Agriculture, as did many of the original personnel. In Poston, many key personnel transferred from the Office of Indian Affairs.

The War Relocation Authority included in its organization chart a Community Analysis section comprised of anthropologists, sociologists, and other social scientists to help the WRA Director manage the centers. The presence of Community Analysts in Washington and in each of the camps was a recognition of the ignorance of most of the WRA staff concerning Japanese cultural traditions and the history of the Japanese in the United States. They had no idea of the psychological strains that relocation would have on these uprooted people. And no one really knew how to "govern" these artificially created communities. The Community Analysts in the centers sent frequent reports to Washington that were translated into useful directives. Insofar as a low priority bureaucracy can respond, the WRA did make an effort to modify its policies, but in the beginning the Administration leaned on the young Americanized English-speaking *nisei*, while ignoring the older, more traditional Japanese-speaking *issei*.

Poston was a particularly studied center. In addition to Community Analysis, John Collier, the Commissioner of Indian Affairs, established a Bureau of Sociological Research. The University of

Opposite page: First sick man at this War Relocation Authority center for evacuees of Japanese ancestry. (National Archives)

California set up the Japanese-American Evacuation and Resettlement Study. All the studies received information from evacuees. Those who cooperated in research inquiries were often suspected of "informing," resulting in unpopularity in the camp. The administrative staff came under research scrutiny, too, although we were unaware of being under a microscope. Whatever conclusions the "experts" reached rarely trickled down to us guinea pigs. We would have welcomed some good advice.

One of Poston's anthropologists, Alexander Leighton, later wrote a detailed book* analyzing how conflict situations should be handled and offering a handy distinction between the two types of administrative personnel—the "stereotype-minded" and the "people-minded." That book and many others since have made clear what factors affected the "governing" of and adaptation within this artificial community.

*Alexander H. Leighton, *The Governing of Men: General Principles and Recommendations Based on Experience at a Japanese Relocation Camp*, Princeton University Press, 1945.

Above: Jim Morikawa sprinkling in an attempt to settle the dust at this War Relocation Authority center for evacuees of Japanese ancestry. (National Archives)

A few definitions may help.

The *issei* were Japan-born aliens, ineligible for naturalization because of U.S. laws against granting citizenship to Orientals. The *nisei*, or second generation, were their American-born children. About 20 percent of the *nisei* were *kibei*, U.S. citizens who had some of their school years in Japan. The *sansei* were third-generation citizens, and most were infants during the years of World War II.

The average age of the alien *issei* men was 60. They had come to America in their youth. After 10 or 15 years, when they felt established and/or had become resigned to remaining in their new country, they sent back to Japan for wives. Photos were exchanged, and soon the "picture brides" arrived. The *issei* women were at least 10 years younger than their husbands. These parents, with hard work, had built a decent living, usually in farming, restaurants and hotels, or small shops. They did not show up on the welfare rolls or in prison. These industrious parents had raised their children with old-fashioned Japanese values: to respect authority, to revere their elders, to esteem education. Two-thirds of their *nisei* children were under 20. Such sons and daughters had never thought of arriving late to school, much less playing truant; they would have felt deeply ashamed to be sent to the principal's office. With their classmates, they pledged allegiance to the flag and succumbed to baseball fever.

Most "whole families" consisted of an *issei* father and mother, with *nisei* children. In spite of the degradation of relocation and bitterness against the treatment of their citizen children, this group of *issei* tended to maintain their loyalty to the United States because their children's future was clearly American.

There were also "split families" whose fathers had been interned in New Mexico or Texas by the Department of Justice. The *issei* mother, with limited English, had faced the sudden uprooting, the forced sale of family possessions, and in camp worried greatly about the future of herself and her *nisei* children. Such mothers often considered a return to Japan as a possible solution.

A third group of *issei* were the bachelors. They had usually worked for other people, didn't own a business or lease land, and had put down no family roots. As they aged into their sixties and seventies, they remembered their Japanese childhood, revered the Emperor, and even believed that someday they would return to Japan. Some believed firmly in Japan's ultimate victory and were the first to ask for repatriation to the fatherland.

As a rule, the *issei* knew some English, but usually not enough to read and write.

The FBI roundup of "dangerous" aliens included many *issei* who had been prominent in their West Coast communities. Their absence resulted in a leadership vacuum in the Relocation Centers. At the outset, the WRA ruled that only citizen *nisei* could serve on the elected Community Councils, although all evacuees over 18 could vote for the Council members. The *issei* could serve as block managers and fill other community positions, but they greatly resented being subordinated to their children.

Among the young *nisei* there were differences, too. Age was the crucial factor. The younger ones were not part of the developing power struggle in the Relocation Center. School and play and fishing in the river kept them busy. Those in their twenties and above worked in the hospital, the schools, or the administrative offices, and saw themselves as completely American. In spite of their having attended Japanese language school outside of regular school hours back on the West Coast, few *nisei* were fluent in Japanese beyond knowing some spoken words.

Many *nisei* were members of the JACL (Japanese American Citizens League), which had testified against evacuation, but, faced with the fact, had urged compliance and cooperation with the U.S. Government. Some 250 *nisei* had come to Poston early as volunteers to help set up "intake" procedures. While these *nisei* worked alongside the staff personnel, their *issei* parents might go for weeks without seeing any Caucasians. Naturally enough, the Administration leaned on these helpful, willing, articulate *nisei*. As a result, some of the older *issei* and Japan-educated *kibei* suspected the favored *nisei* of being informers (*inu*, or dogs).

Other young *nisei*, many from farm backgrounds, had different skills and different hopes from urban *nisei*. In camp they worked in the camouflage net factory, in security and fire prevention, in hog and poultry raising. Their immediate Caucasian "bosses" tended to be the "stereotype-minded" who brought no tolerance to their assignment. Their treatment of the evacuees tended to erode the "patriotism" of the *nisei* they supervised.

The *nisei* whose fathers were interned had good reason to doubt American justice. Those whose fathers were later paroled to join their families in Relocation Centers usually accepted their plight, since their fathers urged them to do so, in spite of their own earlier internment.

A small minority of *nisei* would not work for $16 a month. Idle, bored, hostile, they were a restive element, ripe to be used by others also embittered.

The really wild card was the Japan-educated group called *kibei*. They were usually male, usually the oldest child. These children were sent to Japan to stay with grandparents as a sort of family courtesy, or to benefit from what their *issei* parents considered to be superior education in Japan. The factors affecting *kibei* attitudes were the age they'd been when they were sent to Japan and the length of time they spent there. The young ones who'd spent just a year or two in elementary school were indistinguishable from other *nisei* kids, except in the official records. Those who'd spent several years in high school or college during the 1930s, when Japan was becoming more nationalistic and militaristic, were often persuaded by that indoctrination.

Many *kibei* believed in the invincibility of Japan and scorned the softness and seeming lack of discipline in American culture. These *kibei* acted more Japanese than the older *issei*, who had not been in Japan for many decades. The *kibei* were much less fluent in English than their *nisei* peers and often joined with disaffected *issei*, playing on evacuee fears and dissatisfaction. They spread rumors and tried to keep the community in turmoil. The hard-core *kibei* were "bully boys" who beat up the *nisei* who cooperated with the Administration.

Aside from the ill-advised WRA rule that only the *nisei* could serve on the Community Council, there was little chance of self-government, as long as people remained incarcerated and patrolled by M.P.'s. The camp newspaper, the *Poston Chronicle*, occasionally published controversial articles and reprinted news from outside newspapers. One page was printed in Japanese without censorship, but the newspaper could be suspended at any time by the Project Director.

In spite of good intentions, the WRA staff in Washington and in Centers were afflicted by the father-knows-best syndrome. This paternalistic attitude resulted in policies and directives, without concern for whether those orders were acceptable to the whole community. If the Administration accepted advice at all, it was from the cooperative *nisei*, who constituted a majority of the population, but did not represent the thinking of their elders. The young *nisei* valued American self-expression learned in school, while the older *issei* represented a tradition of consensus. The *issei* further resented the *nisei* for getting all the good, interesting jobs, while the *issei* were assigned the menial work.

The WRA staff was aware that camp life was artificial and could soon lead to an undesirable dependency with ever-lessening ambition. For this reason, the WRA began relocating evacuees out of the camps. Dispersal of evacuees to the East Coast and Middle West would serve several purposes. Since no one knew when the evacuees could return to the West Coast, it was important that the young people continue their education or pursue careers in their chosen fields. These "ambassadors of good will" would make eastern communities able to distinguish the enemy in Japan from the loyal group in the United States. Perhaps after the war, many *nisei* would make their lives away from the West Coast, thus breaking up the pattern of Little Tokyos.

These relocation efforts were not always successful. Each evacuee had to receive "leave clearance" before leaving camp. Because this often took weeks or even months to obtain, an evacuee might have lost the chance at a job or a college scholarship. And, while the WRA saw the Centers as temporary stopping places, the *issei* quietly dug in, determined to stay put and keep families together for the duration.

All of this—the leadership vacuum, the shutting out of experienced *issei* from positions of responsibility, the pushing and pulling between and within generations—seems so clear in hindsight. Scholars working from the camp records recognize at once the factors that made conflict inescapable. Those of us from the lower echelons working in the camps had no such enlightenment.

Opposite page: A scene in Jr. High School - the ninth grade. (National Archives)

School Days

Setting up a camp school system
for thousands of children
created many difficult problems.

In Poston alone there were some 5,300 pupils in kindergarten through the 12th grade, and Poston was only one of the ten Relocation Centers on the U.S. mainland. Wartime shortages of nearly everything affected our ability to obtain school supplies. Poston, at the beginning, was jointly administered by the WRA and the Office of Indian Affairs, so all requisitions had to go through an additional layer of bureaucracy. The slowness of it all made grown men and women weep, and caused prolonged hardships for students waiting endlessly for school supplies.

In Poston we had 100 civil service teacher positions which were never more than 85 percent filled. Evacuee teachers, at times, numbered up to 219. Recruiting outside teachers was slow and the results uneven. For civil service teachers, the pay wasn't bad for 1942—$1,620 per year. (By 1944, when the WRA took over the total administration of Poston from the Office of Indian Affairs, high school teacher salaries increased to $2,000 per year.) Even so, teachers did not rush to come to Relocation Centers. Few teachers outside the West Coast even knew there were such job openings. Appointed teachers came and went, sometimes with breathtaking rapidity due to the living conditions, heat and fear fed by newspapers and radio reports about dangerous enemies within who might rise up and murder us in our beds. Recruitment continued as long as the camps remained open.

The roster of evacuee teachers continually changed as *nisei* teachers left to complete their education at Midwest and Eastern colleges or to join the Army when it accepted Japanese-Americans in 1943.

I had signed up at the regional Indian Bureau office in Chicago to be an Assistant Teacher—a helper, a gofer—to watch and learn, looking toward a bright future day when I would be fully qualified to teach. What a hope! I was immediately ordered to be a teacher, and so I tried to become one.

When school opened in Poston Camp I in October 1942, classes were held in recreation halls scattered all across the camp—three classrooms to a building. Unfortunately, many halls had not yet been partitioned, so chaos reigned.

I was lucky. The Block 35 recreation hall had been partitioned. I had a painted blackboard, but no chalk. There were desks, or rather tables, but no chairs. Some paper and pencils. If you dropped a pencil, it usually fell between the floorboards, never to be seen again. And in the early mornings of November, when the desert winds blew cold and the water froze in the irrigation ditch, the children stood around an oil-can stove outside to thaw their hands before they could even hold a pencil.

And, no books! They didn't arrive until January 1943, three months after classes began.

The science and cooking classrooms, the auto mechanics and woodworking shops were not big enough nor properly equipped; they were not wired for electricity and lacked running water. When the books finally did arrive, learning was by the text alone. Hands-on learning was a distant promise.

Poston lucked out and got surplus typewriters and sewing machines from a military training camp and a National Youth Administration camp, respectively. A Relocation Center in Arkansas acquired three looms and a teacher and thereafter produced magnificent weavings.

The State of California scrapped all their Rugg textbooks in favor of a more conservative series. These old volumes and other castoff books—more than 50,000 of them—were literally shoveled into freight cars and unshoveled in the town of Parker onto trucks to be unloaded in heaps in Poston. The books arrived in a fairly grimy state and were dumped on dusty floors to be picked over through many sweltering hours. Everyone with free time pitched in to sort, repair, or trash the books too battered for salvage. These schoolbooks were truly valuable hand-me-downs.

"My" kids, ninth-graders, brought their own "chairs" to the classroom—assorted boxes to sit on while they listened to "the teacher." The girls, colorful in summer cottons, sat quietly; the boys, with sun-rusted hair, slouched at the back.

I brought along a piece of paper on which to inscribe the pupils' names. I sought inspiration but could come up only with the notion of a spelling bee.

Alas, my desk was near the blackboard, far from the door, where the boys were. Those boys drifted out quietly, but with dispatch. The next morning I moved the desk beside the door, but hadn't a clue what to do next. Ah, a writing assignment! Would you, could you, believe that I told the class to write a paper on "What Democracy Means to Me"?!? And would you believe that those kids wrote serious answers? Some were stumblingly patriotic, some bitter, many understandably confused.

I somehow obtained a list of state offices that could supply information upon request. Each student chose a state and wrote a letter asking for information about the population, natural resources, scenic parks, or whatever category sounded interesting.

Some requests were never answered. West Virginia generously responded to every request. Surely, there must have been some bafflement in state offices. Clerks may not have recognized a Japanese name when they saw it, and where under the sun was the Colorado River Relocation Center, Poston, Arizona? It wasn't on any map. Anyway, when the dozens of pamphlets and fact sheets arrived, we possessed some free "educational materials," albeit a motley collection.

I read to the class from any books or magazines that I could beg, borrow, or buy in the town of Parker, or the students read aloud to the class.

The Core Curriculum teachers were faced with double periods. By combining English and Social Studies, the goal was to strengthen oral and written language skills and learning ability in the course of mastering subject matter, which in turn could be applied to a growth of understanding of personal and community problems, leading ideally to the development of responsible, sensitive citizens for their role in a democracy. Whew!

Miles Cary, the Director of Education, had come to Poston from McKinley High School in Honolulu, where Core Curriculum had been routine for several years. He was a true believer who tried to keep us all at a high level of enthusiasm. "Core Curriculum? A simple concept, very logical, you'll love it." He never lost his commitment, but he did have to admit that not all teachers had the same conviction nor the background necessary to succeed.

His contagious enthusiasm spilled over into other areas. Classrooms without partitions? They'd be ready soon. No furniture?

Don't worry. No books? They'd be along shortly. Not enough teachers? More would come. We soon stopped asking questions.

I don't know how the other Core Curriculum teachers fared, but I kept asking the school office for help and was told to "start where the students are." This meant beginning with Charles Debrill Poston, for whom the camp was named. He'd been a desert pioneer and the first Arizona territorial delegate to Congress. The evacuee teachers may have received some information about him during the training session, but I'd never heard of him. Nor did I know any history of Arizona.

Other school personnel influenced me, especially two school principals from Hawai'i. The Camp I high school principal, less exuberant than the Director, was equally optimistic that we teachers could meet all challenges, and was always available to try to help us over the obstacles. He would prove very important to me as time went by. Later, in my second year in Poston Camp II, the principal would be my "higher authority" and back me up whenever needed.

The Camp I elementary school principal, stocky and stout-hearted, came to Poston from the Indian Service. She didn't care whether pupils were red or yellow or white. She cared only that they be well and kindly taught.

These educators brought high standards and great expectations. More importantly, their doors were always open. They listened, comforted, and helped the teachers—staff or evacuee—when we faltered.

I fumbled and stumbled along until Ann arrived, a very attractive, young blonde from Kansas, with credentials. Now the class was in good hands and I could be her morning "assistant." One afternoon, as I busied myself with clerical work in the principal's office, some evacuee parents came to report that Ann was hitting the children with a ruler and yelling at them. Her tenure had lasted only a matter of days, until she dated a Caucasian M.P. who may or may not have raped her, but surely unhinged her and drove her to bizarre behavior.

The resident "social anthropologist" asked me to have supper with Ann that evening. He didn't explain why. Ann was totally incoherent. She left Poston that night or the next day, under restraint. We later learned that she'd previously spent some time in a Kansas mental hospital. How could her parents let her leave home, especially to such unknown territory as a Relocation Center?

Her replacement, Myrtle, arrived—an older and experienced teacher. Unfortunately, she suffered from sleeping sickness, a malady she'd contracted in Africa. In a few weeks, she also boarded a departing train.

Then came the fourth teacher. By this time, most of the boys were truant and the girls listless. The class attitude was: We've driven out three teachers and we'll do the same to Number Four. This time the students had met their match in quiet Quaker Marydel. She not only saved those teenagers from running amok, but stayed until the camp closed down in 1945.

Not all of the classrooms suffered so much upheaval, but there were other passing problems.

Mrs. M., in her sixties, had recently completed many years as a missionary teacher in Japan. She expected to impress her students with her impeccable Japanese. Since few of the American-educated 12th-graders spoke "her" language, she received blank stares and giggles. Fortunately, Mrs. M. reacted quickly and successfully by speaking equally excellent English. Her ability to converse with the parents meant that she could often head off misunderstandings between school and family.

She also conveyed a deep appreciation of the Japanese culture and respect for the Japanese people. She wrote Japanese characters on the green chalkboard, while explaining the meaning and stressing the beauty of the calligraphy as drawn by artists. She told old *samurai* stories of bravery and loyalty, and spooky tales of hauntings.

Another fascinating mentor, Edythe, wore her red hair braided over her ears in a style that hadn't been seen for a hundred years. But she was a demon for grammar, with a deep knowledge of history and a talent for drama. In class she portrayed such historical figures as Queen Elizabeth and Mary Todd Lincoln. What vivid memories her students must have!

George P. was recruited over the telephone and arrived convinced that he was expected to face some kind of student ROTC activity, rather than Core Curriculum. He changed gears very smoothly. George had a deprecating way of telling funny stories about himself as a way of letting the boys know that being turned down by a girl or dropping a baseball was not the end of the world.

The evacuee teachers must have had their problems, but they didn't air them publicly. I know, from talking to some of their students recently, that the students remember their evacuee teachers more clearly than they do the Caucasian staff teachers. Most of the evacuee teachers were hardly older than their high school students, but they had suffered through the painful uprooting and relocation. They didn't just sympathize with the evacuees, they were evacuees themselves. Consequently, they didn't overreact to the anger and posturing of hostile students.

I'd come to Poston with the impression that the California school system was the best in the country. Maybe so for Caucasian students, but it seemed to me that the *nisei* products of those schools excelled at rote learning and memorizing. They studied hard, got good grades, particularly in math and science, but were not prepared for original thinking, for answering essay questions, or for speaking up in class whether to ask or answer a question. Student government? Most unlikely. There were exceptions to my generalization, but that's the way I saw it.

When Poston students were tested the first year, most scored below the national standard median level. Perhaps the low test scores were due to emotional turmoil, living in a new "home" and attending a new school.

At the end of three years in camp schools, all grade levels were at or above standard medians. English composition and math reasoning, for instance, were low the first year and above grade level by the third. The facts are known, but not the reasons. Perhaps the improvement was due to stabilization of the teaching staff and/or acceptance of camp life? Or perhaps it was the result of a single ethnic group comprising the whole student body and, therefore, having a chance to be class president, the best speller, or queen of the Harvest Festival?

School was not all class work during that first autumn of 1942. With the acute labor shortage caused by the war, the nearby cotton growers desperately needed anyone to pick the crop. The country needed cotton and growers needed workers. The Poston evacuees responded with enthusiasm, picking 36,000 pounds of cotton that year. Students took turns making money for their class treasuries, for special projects, or celebrations. I "chaperoned" some of these prickly excursions. Yes, cotton bolls are sharp! At 80 cents for a humongous bag, it was hard-earned money. I couldn't have made a living that way; the kids outpicked me by about five times. The students enjoyed their brief freedom outside camp—joking and singing as they picked. Before the harvest was completed, the Army called a halt to this mutual-benefit arrangement. We never knew why.

The cotton growers treated Poston students as well as they treated their usual workers who'd found easier, better-paying work in the war industry. The residents of Parker were not so civil. On the first outing, our army truck made a gas-up stop on the way back to camp. The student workers were hot and thirsty, anxious to leap out of the truck for cold Cokes. The gas station owner rushed out. "Stop right there!" The kids couldn't even step down from the truck. The driver brought the Cokes back to the dismayed students.

So much for helping the war effort! The drivers avoided the problem thereafter, filling their tanks in camp. We all drank warm water in the cotton fields after that.

I never learned to love Parker. The barbershop had a large sign in the window: "Japs, keep out, you rats!" A young *nisei* in U.S. Army uniform, one of Merrill's Marauders in Burma, was on his way to visit his parents in Poston. As he walked by the window, the barber rushed out and struck him on the head with what was thought to be a baseball bat.

A young bride-to-be whose family planned a really nice wedding could buy her wedding dress in Parker, but she had to enter the small shop from a side street after regular hours so the townspeople would not harass the shop owner for "trading with the enemy."

I took no comfort from the fact that the town treated the Mohave Indians with the same contempt as they did the evacuees.

The administrative personnel had the freedom to drive away, but, with rationed gas, had no place to go, except to Parker. The M.P.'s guarding Poston had their "R&R" in Parker. Therefore, the Parker merchants in town raked in the dollars. The two bars, two restaurants, the hardware and drug stores, as well as the movie house never had it so good.

Some of us did go to Parker on occasional Saturday nights. One bar catered to the Parker Dam workers and the police and firemen from Poston. We teachers patronized the other bar called the Corral. The heavy-handed bartender mixed a mean Old Fashioned and kept the jukebox turned up loud. The dance floor always had a few regulars. In sheer self-defense, I learned to enjoy western music.

Next door to the bar was Ma's, a counter restaurant serving chili about as hot as I could take. I rarely shopped in the stores, preferring to make any necessary purchases on rare trips to Phoenix or by mail order. I never entered the movie theatre.

Above: Sign on a barbershop in Parker, Arizona near the Colorado River Relocation Center. (National Archives)

Pressures Mount

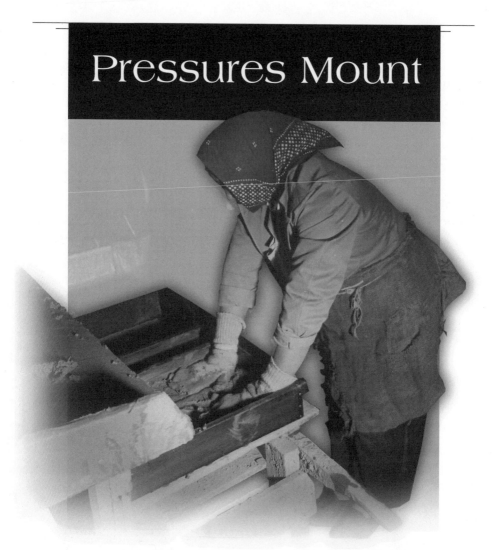

The opening of school had been a relief
to all of us. Teachers could get on with their proper
work. Parents found reassurance that the
Administration would deliver on its promises.

Elementary school children welcomed a pattern to their days, while high school students could again hope to graduate some day.

From May of 1942, when the first evacuees had arrived, throughout the summer, the Administration had worked quickly to provide recreation and hobby activities. A baseball diamond appeared here and a basketball court there. A stage arose where amateur *Kabuki* players could perform, along with concerts and pageants. Nearby was space where *sumo* wrestlers could grunt and groan. Eventually even a swimming pool was dug. Poston was lucky to have a river full of fish, and the desert offered driftwood and native stones to collect for crafts.

But for an ethnic society committed to education, the existence of schools gave confidence to the community. Now, in November 1942, the Project Engineer posted plans for more permanent school buildings. Mothers and fathers joined the work force to make hundreds of thousands of adobe bricks. These well-designed adobe buildings proved serviceable and handsome. When the camp was vacated, most of these structures were cannibalized for bricks to build houses in the town of Parker. What was left—the dirt and straw—reverted to the earth from which they came.

In October 1942, aside from making bricks, many of the adult evacuees were already at work, receiving $12, $16, or $19 a month, depending on the skill level of the jobs. All kinds of jobs needed doing—clerical work in the offices, medical, nursing and pharmacy work in the hospital, and jobs in security and the fire department. Within the community, evacuees ran the mess halls, block management, the cooperative stores, and the entire range of needed services, such as shoe repair, dry cleaning, barbering and hair dressing—just about everything for a town of 10,000 people.

Young *nisei* were hired for seasonal jobs outside of camp, mainly to harvest sugar beets in Utah and Idaho. From the ten camps, some 10,000 people helped to save the year's much-needed sugar beet crop, yielding 265,000,000 pounds of sugar. The evacuees looked forward to the chance to leave camp and earn good, prevailing wages. Some were disillusioned by the prejudice that they encountered. A few met slippery

Opposite page: Adobe factory. A woman worker placing mortar in adobe form. (National Archives)

Above: Adobe factory drying racks. (National Archives)

practices—smaller paychecks than promised, high prices in company stores, and unexpected charges for housing. An unproven rumor that harvest workers were being systematically murdered thinned the ranks in later years, even though the hard cash was tempting.

To support the war effort in Poston, a factory was built to manufacture camouflage nets, with the proceeds benefiting the hospital and the evacuees. To lessen the need to bring in food supplies, evacuees raised hogs and chickens.

The Japanese heritage of successful small farming continued. "Official" truck gardens received water from irrigation ditches that wound through the camp, fed by the Colorado River. "Unofficial" block gardens appeared near the latrines and laundry buildings, where water was plentiful. Individual gardeners grew little plots of cherished culinary items outside their "apartments," watering them by pot and pitcher.

Manzanar in California stood on truly hard-scrabble land. The evacuees there produced enough vegetables for their own use and sent the surplus to other Relocation Centers or sold it to the local markets.

Those not employed turned to creative pursuits. Here and there was a carefully-raked garden of stones or a small pool of carp. Such pools softened the landscape, reflecting clouds in the day and the moon and stars at night, providing spiritual nourishment in the barren landscape. Over and above the drive to make living quarters bearable rose the compulsion to create beauty out of ugliness.

Women in their forties and fifties who had worked on the farm, in the restaurant, or at home raising children now had leisure time to fill. Mrs. Tanaka always liked to make paper flowers. Mrs. Yamamoto, in her youth, had taken a class in flower arranging. Mrs. Kato knew how to embroider and knit, while Miss Sakamoto was an expert in drafting patterns. Mr. Higa used his skilled fingers to carve wooden birds copied from an old Audubon book. Mr. Sato demonstrated the basics of calligraphy. These self-appointed teachers soon drew eager learners.

As time passed, the Administration "institutionalized" many of these informal groups by allocating space and providing materials. Other groups stayed small and private. One stone carver might attract only one or two people, or a jeweler might have a single enthusiast.

The creative energy and eagerness to do something with hand and mind overcame all obstacles. Artisans who had no tools made their own. Metal strips were salvaged from packing cases, wire from surplus window screening. The earliest finished projects were utilitarian—wheelbarrows and furniture, then toys and household shrines. Even canes could be carved or covered with rattlesnake skin!

The Arizona desert yielded agate, quartz, petrified wood, even turquoise to polish and carve. Simple rocks were painted as characters in old folk tales. The environs around Relocation Centers in Arkansas offered a variety of wood for carving or selected for shape, grain and color to form *kobu*, which means "wood as found."

In addition to regular *ikebana* flower arrangements—of leaves if there were no flowers—the ingenious people formed *bon-kei* (miniature landscapes of sand on a tray) or *sui-seki* (stones watered until coated with moss to shape mountains or islands) for dish gardens.

Some painters preferred traditional themes such as cranes and plum blossoms, while others focused on the immediate landscape of mountains or mesa, cactus, or the camp life around them.

Musicians crafted their own drums, *samisen* (guitars), and *koto* (zithers), and joined orchestral groups. Theatrical troupes formed to present all types of Japanese drama, including puppet shows.

Art and hobby shows, concerts, and plays became regular events.

On the surface, Poston and the other camps were transformed into productive communities of industry, villages of serenity. Within months, some families had changed blocks in order to be near friends from their home community. Newlyweds usually set up housekeeping where neither bride nor groom had previously resided and settled into a new "neighborhood." Individuals had transferred out of one camp and into another to reunite their families. Many alien *issei* who had been interned in Lordsburg, New Mexico, or Crystal City, Texas, were now "paroled" and joined their families in relocation camps. Parents participated in the PTA, while their children enrolled in the Scouts, Girl Reserves, and the Junior Red Cross. Students were part of the National Honor Society and made posters for charitable activities such as the Christmas Seals and March of Dimes. Many young people found pen pals across the country, usually students in schools from which the staff teachers had come.

Churches—Catholic, Protestant, Buddhist—held regular services. At first, services had to be held in English, but that ruling was later relaxed. Festivals were observed—Girl's Day and Boy's Day and the *bon-odori* dances to honor the dead. Scattered throughout were poetry societies, tea ceremonies, and men gathered to play *go* (checkers), using pebbles for counters.

Above: Children and their parents who once attended the Catholic Church of Father Clement, Maryknoll Priest, are now reestablished in homes back in California or throughout the Middle West and the East. (National Archives)

As idealistic as all these activities may sound, these camps were not real communities. With no possibility of self-government, how could there be reality? Dr. H., the Poston Director of Education beginning in 1943, called the setup "a paternalistic bureaucracy, without normal civic, economic and family responsibilities, in a ghetto type of geographic segregation." Beneath the illusory surface, people harbored large resentments and small irritations, aggravated by the daily diet of rumor.

Camp life for the *issei* men was a shattering experience. These proud patriarchs were profoundly unhappy to lose family control. No longer the breadwinners, they now possessed no sense of self-determination, not even any self-respect. They held little confidence in the future. Were they not actually prisoners of war? Would they be deported to Japan? What would become of their children who were U.S. citizens? After decades in America, the *issei* world was no longer a Japanese world. They looked back more to the West Coast than to Japan. They wanted their children to attend college, but, during these uncertain times, they were reluctant to have the family break up.

The jobs in camp at low wages could not replace their own farms, stores, or restaurants. Furthermore, the meager pay they received was often late and sometimes short. The men who did the dirty work of collecting trash and raising hogs at $12 a month resented those in clean jobs in schools and administrative offices earning $19 a month. Inexperienced *nisei* managed the camp store, while experienced *issei* served as janitors. The camp jobs served the needs of the relocation center, but not the skills and desires of the men. They resented the Caucasian supervisors who often knew less than they themselves did. They particularly objected to the "child council," as they called the Community Council, comprised of young *nisei* who lacked experience or expertise.

The Japanese American Citizens League continued to pressure the Federal government to open the Armed Forces to *nisei* volunteers who wished to demonstrate their loyalty to the U.S. Many *issei* bachelors and *kibei* malcontents were infuriated by the League's efforts to show loyalty

Opposite page top: Evacuees of Japanese ancestry fish for carp in the canal on the northwest side of this War Relocation Authority center. Inset: A young evacuee of Japanese ancestry entertains her fellow evacuees with a demonstraton of her tap dancing ability. This was one number in an outdoor musical show. (National Archives) to a country that seemingly didn't want them and had treated them so unfairly.

Even the news was untrustworthy. The official camp newspaper, the *Poston Chronicle*, was written by evacuees, but under the supervision of the Reports Officer, and often published "managed" news. The "rags" from California, particularly the *Los Angeles Times*, fostered fear and hate. Rumors of all kinds spread fast.

There were often shortages of all kinds of food. Had the whole transportation of the nation broken down? Was the food supply deliberately cut off in order to starve the evacuees? Was there a deliberate attempt to poison them?

More plausible than the poisoning rumor was the widely-circulated story that administrative warehousemen were diverting supplies of meat and sugar to sell on the black market. Nothing says a rumor can't be true. An investigation actually proved the charges and some workers were fired. The communal eating in the mess halls continued to cause unhappiness, as conventional family meals were impossible.

Another rumor suggested that going to the hospital meant certain death, and that the dead were spirited out under cover of darkness. Alas, there were miscarriages and premature births among the evacuees, and deaths that might have been prevented in a better hospital. The 250-bed hospital was not well designed or fully equipped. There seemed to be an epidemic of appendectomies and a high incidence of peptic ulcers. The administrative doctor, Dr. P., was unpopular for double-dosing the staff for typhoid, and his brusque manner did not endear him to anyone. However, he performed no surgery on the evacuees. A majority of the hospital staff of physicians, nurses, and pharmacists were evacuees who did their very best. Complaints about rude treatment or poor ambulance service were due to personnel shortages and overwork, rather than to discrimination.

Almost anything could provoke complaint. All packages were opened and inspected by the Military Police; it didn't matter whether the package was sent by an outside friend or Sears Roebuck. When an evacuee was expecting a package that never arrived, had the WRA staff withheld it? Or stolen it?

Above: Toshi Katano, at work in her beauty shop. (National Archives)

In November, the temperatures at night dropped down to freezing, but the stoves had not arrived. Bonfires were a common sight. Like-minded *issei* men often gathered to grumble—about the clothing allowances that were not forthcoming, or the inadequate schools with "progressive" notions and unqualified teachers.

And now that the desert winds blew cold, some transferees from northern centers to Poston complained that the barracks in Granada or Tule Lake were more weatherproof. Actually, there were differences among camps according to the demands of climate. Postonites, for instance, could assert that only their camp had double-roofing to protect against the heat.

Issei aliens "paroled" to join their families in Relocation Centers might report that they'd had better housing and better food in the internment camps in New Mexico or Texas. True or not, the Poston evacuees believed that the U.S. Government treated the "enemy" better than it did its own citizens. The Spanish government, as a neutral nation, monitored the treatment of Japanese internees and directed complaints to the U.S. Departments of State and Justice, which sometimes effected changes.

The *issei* got their national news from the Japanese language newspapers in Denver and Salt Lake City, where Japanese-Americans were "living free." From these papers, the *issei* learned about the continuing prejudice on the West Coast. Ironically, the groups that had pressured the U.S. Government to incarcerate everyone of Japanese descent on the basis of possible risk from espionage and sabotage, now used the evacuation as proof that all were therefore disloyal and traitorous. This propaganda was steady and intense to insure that no Japanese would ever return to their home communities on the West Coast.

Specific grievances expressed to the block managers were forwarded to the Community Council, which, in turn, submitted them to the Project Directors. He and his staff did not always quickly sense underlying attitudes. A complaint about food shortages was likely to be answered with an official statement that the whole country suffered from shortages. A suggestion that the problem might be caused by inefficient distribution or, worse, black marketing by administrative personnel, might be interpreted as personal criticism.

Continuing delays and nondelivery of essentials aggravated everyone. The evacuees and administrative personnel tended to forget that the whole nation faced shortages of all kinds. Textbook publishers fought to get paper, shoe manufacturers were short of leather, and appliance manufacturers lacked steel, chrome, and rubber. On the "outside," rationing became a way of life—sugar, meat, shoes, everything. Housewives saved and returned grease to the butcher. Smokers stood in long lines for Fatima and Raleigh cigarettes, or rolled their own. Nylon stockings? Forget it. A whole new "industry" of stocking repair emerged. Trading ration stamps developed into a fine art. Black marketing was rampant.

"Inside" the camp, the food was not great, but adequate. No one needed fancy shoes or scarce nylons. But shortages on the outside didn't reconcile the evacuees to their own deprivation.

Occasionally, the staff did do something right. Poston remained the only Relocation Center that did not, in November of 1942, have barbed wire around the camp, only some remote fencing to control the straying Indian cattle.

There were no manned guard towers with searchlights sweeping over the camp at night. The seeming openness did not spell freedom. Any fence, emphasized by M.P.'s at the gate, bordered on one side by the wide Colorado River, otherwise surrounded by hostile desert, spelled incarceration.

Still, Poston seemed fractionally less restricted than the other camps. The absence of confining measures had evidently been an oversight or a postponement. In November 1942, word circulated that the lack of barbed wire would soon be "remedied." The Project Attorney, Ted, was one of the first to hear the news. Ted, a tense man dedicated to the protection of evacuee rights, heard the news about a new fence. A small impromptu meeting of the "people-minded" staff was held. We protested the fencing and demanded action. Someone suggested summoning the Project Director. He came, he listened.

The guard towers and barbed wire fence did not go up.

We prided ourselves on our small victory. Over the months, the restrictions in the other centers lessened. The searchlights went out, the guard towers stood empty, and the evacuees could roam their desolate surroundings outside the barbed wire. However, the fences and guard towers, symbols of incarceration, remained in place.

Above: Community Council and secretaries of Poston.

The following anonymous poem circulated in Poston. The sentiment is sincere, even though Poston had only a wire fence to keep out the Indian cattle, and no guard towers.

THAT DAMNED FENCE

They've sunk the posts deep into the ground
They've strung out wires all the way around.
With machine gun nests just over there
And sentries and soldiers everywhere.

We're trapped like rats in a wired cage,
To fret and fume with impotent rage;
Yonder whispers the lure of the night,
But that DAMNED FENCE assails our sight.

We seek the softness of the midnight air,
But that DAMNED FENCE in the floodlight glare
Awakens unrest in our nocturnal quest,
And mockingly laughs with vicious jest.

With nowhere to go and nothing to do,
We feel terrible, lonesome and blue:
That DAMNED FENCE is driving us crazy,
Destroying our youth and making us lazy.

Imprisoned in here for a long, long time,
Now we're punished—though we've committed no crime,
Our thoughts are gloomy and enthusiasm damp,
To be locked up in a concentration camp.

Loyalty we know, and patriotism we feel,
To sacrifice our utmost was our ideal,
To fight for our country, and die perhaps;
But we're here because we happen to be Japs.

We all love life, and our country best,
Our misfortune to be here in the west,
To keep us penned behind that DAMNED FENCE,
Is someone's notion of NATIONAL DEFENSE!

Day by Day

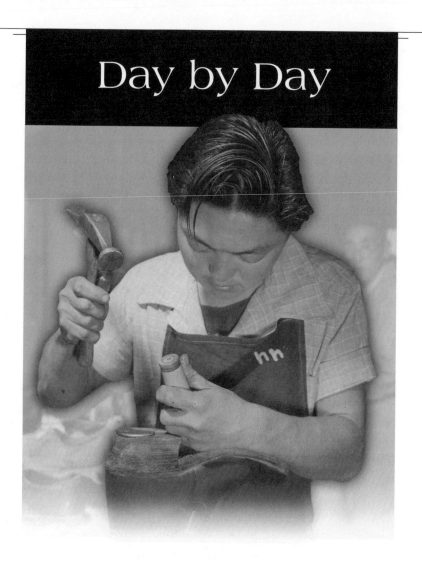

As a staff member,
I could come and go freely.

Certainly the "people-minded" and "stereotype-minded" personnel had disagreements, so we associated with those who agreed with us. The Project Director of Poston luckily tended to be "people-minded."

I visited only one other Relocation Center when I "chaperoned" some transferees south to the Gila River Relocation Center near Phoenix. It was dusk when I arrived, and I left early in the morning. I recall the red-roofed, whitewashed barracks. This was the "pretty" camp where Eleanor Roosevelt spent a well-supervised day and reported back to the President that all was well. When my mother visited Phoenix and read the scurrilous accounts about Poston, she wondered why I wasn't at Gila River, which had received such good news reports. If it was good enough for Mrs. Roosevelt...

I don't know how the transferees into and out of Gila River compared it to Poston, but I was shocked. At Gila River, the evacuees waiting on tables were quick, efficient, and virtually mute. My administrative tablemates seemed by attitude and policy to be committed to avoiding any socializing with the evacuees. I was relieved to get back to unpretty, but friendlier, Poston. No one claimed that we were having a love feast, but we talked to each other and we had no policy dictating that we couldn't.

Of course, the Security people, being "stereotype-minded," wanted no fraternization and disapproved of those of us who did. They expected trouble; they seemed to lust for it. Working for Security was not a favorite job assignment for the evacuees. They could expect nothing but general contempt or overt insults.

Some Security men bragged loudly about weapons, leading to the rumor that the administrative staff was armed and ready to attack at the least provocation. Again, a partial truth. A Security employee in one of the male staff barracks kept a trunkful of rifles, pistols, and probably much more. Each man in that barracks was offered a view of the cache and invited to help himself if trouble arose. I do not know whether this alarming "treasure" was ever confiscated, but this redneck never, thank God, got his chance at target practice.

Opposite page: Shoe repair shop. (National Archives)

The teachers, administrative and evacuee, attended regular faculty meetings. We consulted back and forth to solve problems with equipment, curriculum, and student adjustment.

There were social get-togethers in camp where evacuees and administrative personnel got acquainted. The *issei* stood back and bowed. We were equally ill at ease and couldn't bow as gracefully. The *nisei*, with a foot in two worlds, took over. To break the formal standoff, they set up excruciatingly painful parlor games such as passing an empty matchbox from nose to nose and other kiddie high jinks. It worked! It's hard to be unfriendly when you're giggling.

Few of us were aware of the convoluted differences among the evacuees, but we, too, were often confused by orders from above. Because Poston sat on Indian land, we served two masters. The Office of Indian Affairs shared responsibility with the War Relocation Authority in all decision making. The Commissioner of Indian Affairs would come to Poston one week to talk about permanence and how wonderful the camp would be in 15 years. The Director of the WRA would arrive a week later, urging the evacuees to relocate eastward to jobs or colleges as fast as possible. We were all perplexed.

The continuing negative attitudes reported in newspapers and on the radio disheartened us. Even though we were not fully aware of the depth of discontent among the evacuees, we were conscious of conflicts and feared any incident which might inflame racist attitudes outside of camp.

Any spark might set off an explosion. In mid-November 1942, such a spark was struck at Poston I.

Opposite page: Poston, Arizona. Site #3. Burning brush to clear more land. (National Archives)

The Poston Protest and Strike

Late on the night of Saturday, November 14, a man asleep in a bachelor barracks was severely beaten by a group of unidentified men. This wasn't the first beating in camp. Usually *kibei* and sometimes bitter *nisei* beat up other *nisei* suspected of "consorting with the enemy" by cooperating with the Administration, perhaps telling tales about their fellow evacuees. Such previous occurrences had not proved so serious, nor did they have such unexpected consequences.

Within a very short time, the evacuee police rounded up some 50 suspects to be interviewed by the Chief of Internal Security and the Reports Officer. Of those interviewed, only two were detained in the camp jail. No charges were filed and no one seemed to know why these two had been singled out. The FBI was called in.

All three—the victim and the two who were arrested—were *kibei*, American citizens with some years of schooling in Japan.

The victim had been a rice broker in California with a questionable reputation. He was suspected of sharp practice in business dealings and of abusing his wife and her family, and even of giving innocent names to the authorities after Pearl Harbor to settle some personal grudges.

Both suspects were 27-year-old single men. Suspect One had completed high school in Japan and attended the University of Southern California for two years. He spoke fluent English and was well liked by everyone who knew him.

Suspect Two spoke little English and was not widely known in camp. While in Japan, he had attained the high rank of Fourth Grade in judo and had taught judo in California. In Poston he had set up a Judo Club, which by November was under the supervision of the Department of Adult Education.

Friends and relatives of the suspects gathered at the jail, demanding their release. Supporters from the blocks where the suspects lived soon followed. Their great fear was that the authorities would take the suspects out of camp, since only misdemeanors could be tried in camp. Felonies had to be tried in a state court, and the evacuees had no confidence that the suspects could have a fair trial in an Arizona court.

No one expressed much interest in the victim beyond remarking that he deserved the beating.

The scene was set. No one could predict the outcome. Emotions and personalities, government power, and community attitudes would clash or compromise. How would the drama play out?

While the FBI investigated, meetings were held in the blocks where the men lived. On Tuesday, several *issei* were delegated to call upon the Project Director to attest to the suspects' good character and to offer evidence of their innocence. The Project Director referred them to the

FBI representatives, who refused to release the men until the official investigation was completed.

Supporters held meetings that night in at least six blocks to discuss what to do next. The leadership came primarily from the older *issei*. For the time being, supporters agreed to demonstrate in front of the jail to prevent removal of the suspects.

Wednesday proved to be a very long day for everyone concerned. A second delegation presented the Project Director with a petition with 110 signatures from one block, a respectful request for release of the men, and a second offer to provide proof of innocence. Once again, they were referred to the FBI, only to be turned away.

At mid-morning, both the Project Director and the Associate Project Director left Poston to attend a War Relocation Authority meeting in Salt Lake City, apparently unaware of the strong feelings in camp. The Assistant Director became the Acting Director. He had not been present when the delegations had presented their demands for release and was quite unprepared for the responsibility he had inherited.

Two other key people were absent at the same time—the Project Attorney and the *nisei* Chairman of the Community Council. The Project Attorney might have clarified the legal issues and insisted that charges be brought or the suspects released. The Council Chairman might have served as an interpreter between the Japanese-speaking *issei* and the Administration, explaining why the *issei* felt powerless and frustrated. Without these key people, the "incident" deteriorated rapidly.

At noon, representatives from the demonstrators went block to block announcing a general strike to begin the next day. Everyone was urged to assemble at the jail immediately to show support for the suspects. Most of the evacuees didn't know the men or why they were being held, yet hundreds, and then thousands, of evacuees did show up—some to grumble about their own grievances, many for want of anything better to do.

Japanese flags and banners appeared. Hand-drawn posters went up depicting the two in jail as martyrs and caricaturing those who cooperated with the Administration as *inu* (dogs, meaning informers). Nearby, amplified militant Japanese music played insistently.

Rumors spread that Suspect One would be tried for murder even though the victim was still alive.

Positions were being defined. The *kibei* who despised America recognized an opportunity to cause trouble. The *issei*, pushed aside from positions of leadership, hoped to regain authority. Restless *nisei*, resentful of incarceration, perceived a chance to express their dissatisfaction with life in this artificial community.

The hospital was considered neutral territory, so the Community Council and the *issei* Advisory Board met there to plan strategy. The Acting Director arrived unexpectedly. He'd been down talking to the crowd, asking them to disperse and urging them to trust the camp Administration and the FBI to see that justice was done. Since his words had little effect, he asked the Council to be responsible for making the wishes of the people known in proper form and warned that large gatherings were dangerous to the community.

The evacuees present told the Acting Director about the two earlier meetings with the Project Director and the FBI. The Chairman of the *issei* Board insisted that the suspects be released immediately. The release, he said, would not interfere with the FBI investigation since the two men would remain in camp. Only then would the crowd disperse.

The Acting Director refused to release the men. He told the Council that the FBI promised that the two would not be taken out of camp before the following Monday.

The Council Vice Chairman, a very "Americanized" young *nisei*, demanded that the Administration grant real, not token, self-government to the evacuees. With such self-determination, the suspects could then be released. The Acting Director refused.

The Council members responded by resigning. The *issei* Advisory Board also resigned. Later in the day, all the block managers resigned. There was now no official "government" in camp. The Administration received word that there would be a general strike of all evacuee employees the following day, Thursday.

The Administration staff met to discuss the problem, with FBI and Army representatives present. Only then did the staff become fully aware of the situation. The "stereotype-minded" staff—the Fiscal

Officer, the Chief Administrative Officer, the Supply Officer, and the Reports Officer, among others—were convinced that the whole affair was an organized pro-Axis plot aimed at destroying property and discrediting the government. They preferred to believe in a plot rather than to recognize the general malaise in camp. Nor did they recognize how their own open contempt for the evacuees might have contributed to evacuee hostility. Moreover, they resented the attitude of the evacuee spokesmen.

The Army was willing to move in, if called upon to disperse the crowd, but made it clear that, if they came in, they would take complete charge for as long as necessary.

The "people-minded" staff did not see the protest as a plot, but as the result of general unhappiness. They felt that delay would be better than aggravating the situation. Calling in the M.P.'s to stop the demonstration would drive the leaders underground. If a strike occurred, the evacuees could not be forced to work.

The buck stopped with the Acting Director. The risk was his, along with the responsibility. If he took the easy way out and called in the Army, no one could blame him. But he appeared to doubt that he could trust the M.P.'s. If they waved their guns around or shot someone, it would be disastrous for Poston and for the other camps after the newspapers got through sensationalizing the story. Any lingering evacuee trust would be destroyed. On the other hand, failure to call in the M.P.'s might risk property damage. He'd be blamed if a single fire was set or one person got hurt. Even staff members who now supported him would probably end up blaming him.

He made his decision. He refused to call in the troops, but asked them to patrol outside Camp I, to guard the motor pool, and stop any unauthorized travel between Camp I and the other two camps. In spite of this agreement, an M.P. weapon carrier and a jeep entered camp instead of patrolling outside. The Acting Director had to call the commanding officer twice to get them out.

Community leaders set up an emergency committee, consisting of two representatives from each block. This group of 72 leaders included 20 members from the old *issei* Advisory Board, 12 from the disbanded Community Council, 5 block managers, and others who were new to community leadership.

During a long, loud meeting, hot heads and cool ones made many speeches. Long after midnight, a small Emergency Executive Council of Twelve was designated—one representative from each four blocks, plus three other members. There were eleven *issei* and one *kibei*. The *nisei* who had constituted the earlier Council were squeezed out, even though they supported the strike. The 72 original emergency committee members used their influence to reach out into the whole community to pull in varied groups that began to work together. A truly representational structure was developing.

Each block sent pickets out in shifts and the kitchen provided meals for the night shift. Twenty young men were charged with maintaining law and order, patrolling the camp to prevent vandalism and violence. Another group supervised and distributed food to the mess halls.

In the meantime, a late-hour delegation from the Emergency Executive Council informed the Administration that the general strike would begin on the following day, but that essential functions would continue—food delivery, garbage collection, the hospital and the schools, internal security, and fire protection. The delegates guaranteed that there would be no violence.

The Acting Director left the Administration headquarters to walk through the crowd around the jail, a tall and lonely figure in the flickering light of the fires. He knew hundreds of the evacuees by sight, yet most of those wandering among the fires were *issei* he had never seen before. No one among the crowd welcomed him, but none confronted him with overt hostility. The Internal Security staff presented at least an outward appearance of neutrality, which provided some reassurance.

On Strike Day, Thursday, a few evacuees showed up in the administrative offices, but they were sent back into their side of camp. The Administration did not want any evacuee to be wrongly accused of fraternizing with the enemy or, worse, suspected of "informing."

Work stopped in the camouflage net factory, at the adobe-brick making, in the hog and chicken farming, and on the "official" truck gardens and, of course, in the administrative offices, where evacuees ordinarily performed all types of work.

The FBI announced that they could not continue their investigation and would withdraw. They did not insist that the Acting Director hold the prisoners; he could release them within camp if he wished.

Since there was no official "government" in Camp I, a delegation was recruited from Camps II and III to serve as mediators. They advocated a trial within Poston rather than in an Arizona court, since the offense had nothing to do with the State. But, because the action constituted a felony, WRA policy required state jurisdiction.

The Acting Director was willing to release Suspect One but not Suspect Two. The delegation rejected that suggestion and withdrew from mediation.

On the afternoon of that gray and windy day, the Acting Director met with the newly-elected committee. Heated exchanges ensued, but overall a fair semblance of calm prevailed. The committee reported the same general grievances and insisted that both suspects be released pending trial in camp—exactly what the delegation from Camps II and III had asked. They received the same answer.

On Friday the sheriff of Yuma County arrived to review the cases. He expressed willingness to file charges, but did not insist.

The Acting Director and some of his aides were actually leaning toward a trial in camp and obtained the approval of the Indian Bureau, the War Department and the WRA. He seemed more and more impressed with the unity and leadership among the evacuees and said he hoped that it might continue when the strike ended.

The Emergency Executive Council of Twelve seemed to fear losing their importance. They became secretive about the negotiations. Apparently they wished to be the only group in contact with the Administration, hoping they could demonstrate that they alone had achieved a settlement on their terms. They greatly resented the Acting Director's public announcement that he would release Suspect One, an announcement they had hoped to make.

While the two sides continued to meet, attitudes in the community were changing. The *nisei* resented the escalating militant stance of the vocal protesters and tore down the posters of flags and dogs. Those in control of selecting records to play over the loudspeaker began to intersperse popular American songs with the Japanese music. Many turned away from the Emergency Executive Council's efforts to maintain secrecy and gain power. Others were simply bored with the protest and preferred to be back on their jobs.

Early on Sunday morning—three days after the strike began— the Project Director and the Associate Director returned from their WRA meeting in Salt Lake City. Throughout the strike, they had been unreachable by the Acting Director. They listened to the Project Attorney, who had also returned, and urged a show of indifference that would cause delay and prevent any gains to the leaders. Thus they hoped the strike would fall apart.

Meetings with the Emergency Executive Council continued on Monday. Suspect Two appeared with his chosen evacuee lawyer and asked for a trial, not a release based on a people's petition. The Council presented their demands; the Administration countered with theirs. The proposals were close enough to make a settlement possible.

The Administration agreed that there would be a reshuffling of the whole work force to insure better job distribution and to improve work efficiency. Most importantly, a workable self-government would include the older, experienced *issei*.

The evacuees would assume the responsibility of policing the community and ending gang activities and beatings.

The Project Director gave the Emergency Council the responsibility of carrying out the agreement. He further authorized the release of Suspect Two for trial by the camp Judicial Commission.

Thus ended the "Poston Incident," as it was officially termed. In the evening the pickets and several thousand others gathered to listen to the Project Director and the Emergency Council. After scattered applause, everyone returned to their "home" barracks.

By morning, all the protest signs had been removed and the area swept clean by the evacuees, leaving no trace of the recent disturbance.

How the Strike Looked to Us

On our side of the firebreak,
the strike was unsettling, of course,
but not very clearly understood.

Above: Members of the police department carving clubs. (National Archives)

In the few months I'd been in Poston, I'd become peripherally aware of tensions between the older alien *issei* and the young citizen *nisei*, between the *nisei* and Japan-educated *kibei*, between the *issei* bachelors and *issei* fathers, within families, and among friends. I did not, could not, have a visceral understanding of what these tensions meant, hour by hour, day after day.

Beyond my conception was the grimness of living four, five, even eight in one room, with neighbors on every side, quarreling, interfering, just being there. No place to be alone, to be quiet.

From Sunday, November 15, when the two suspects were jailed, through Wednesday, the demonstrators, sympathizers, and the merely curious had gathered in growing numbers near the jail. At night the pickets had built numerous small fires against the chilly air. In the dark we could look across the wide firebreak to see those fires burning, with black silhouettes huddled around for warmth. Figures moved away, others appeared, as new demonstrators came to relieve those already there. The public address system carried Japanese music, blowing toward us and away as the wind blew and died—all night long.

Most of us on the staff side were not privy to the deliberations; some became increasingly nervous.

I can only speak for myself when I say that I never felt threatened by the evacuees. It seemed to me that most of the teachers recognized that the anti-Administration sentiment was not directed toward individual teachers. Threats and beatings were within the evacuee community—*kibei* against JACL members, or other one-to-one hostilities.

I did fear that a small spark could ignite a firestorm—for example, some unforgivable insult from an administrative staff member to an evacuee which would necessitate an angry response, or an *issei-nisei* quarrel that could lead to violence.

Underlying that feeling was the dread that the Army would then be called in. Our personal and communal effort would be wasted, and 110,000 misused people would be further victimized.

When the strike actually began on Thursday, the schools were to open, but the teachers were told that they need not hold classes if they felt at all frightened. The evacuee teachers showed up, of course, and, as far as I know, so did all the administrative teachers. The only real concern was for the classes in the block adjoining the jail where the crowd assembled.

Perhaps Miss J. was the one who worried everyone; her classroom was in that block. A gray-haired, straight-standing woman, she was dedicated to teaching her sixth-graders up to and beyond their capabilities. As was her custom, she marched from the Administration quarters, waving the American flag. The crowd fell away. Her students may have been edgy, but she was not. She had the boys and girls line up outside the classroom, lifted her flag, and began, "I pledge allegiance..." The student voices rose from a mumble to an affirmative ending, "with liberty and justice for all."

The pickets turned away to form low-voiced groups, while class went on as usual. Parents were probably glad that the school kept open and the children were in such firm hands.

The Acting Director met with a larger number of the staff to go through more wrangling. He received a vote of confidence from welfare and education and other community service employees, but indignation about "mollycoddling" from the prejudiced.

The crowds continued to assemble around the jail. The makeshift signs with block numbers had given way to banners more suggestive of the Japanese flag. At sunup, the demonstrators let forth with the loud battle cry *"Banzai!"* and some of the *kibei* appeared increasingly militant. Symbols were pasted on nearby walls—of dogs (informants), a martyred man, and painted Japanese flags.

Near the jail a stage had been set up. The entertainment was martial music, loudly magnified. As time passed, there were skits and dance performances, and an evening movie to keep the crowd interested.

On Friday night a school dance was held in a mess hall, chaperoned by teachers and the Camp I high school principal. The girls wore pleated skirts and saddle shoes. Except for a few dudes in zoot suits, sporting ducktail haircuts, most of the boys appeared in slacks and shirts. The phonograph played the usual wartime pop music from "The Jersey Bounce" to "Don't Sit Under the Apple Tree." It could have been anywhere in the U.S. It wasn't.

I saw a nervous *issei* approach one of the *nisei* teachers and draw him away from the noise of the music. After a few minutes of conversation, the teacher talked to the principal. The *issei* had requested that the dance be canceled to avoid trouble. The principal made the announcement. There were some groans, but the kids broke up peaceably and went off into the night, talking and singing.

We did not realize that some were already wearying of the strike. The young *nisei* resented the Japanese flags and tore some off the walls. A few hot-headed *issei* wanted to burn buildings or go on a hunger strike, but more voices spoke for moderation.

By Saturday night, the flags were down. The Japanese music was interspersed with current popular American songs. In contrast to an earlier group which had refused to unload anything but food, a new volunteer group offered to unload any and everything. There was a lot of *issei-nisei* friction among the professional hospital staff, but they were all opposed to the strike, since it might jeopardize their futures. The *nisei* came more and more frequently at night to report to trusted friends on the administrative staff.

By the following Thursday the strike was over. Both suspects were out of jail. The Emergency Council of Twelve now bore the responsibility of "keeping the peace." The bonfires and night music remain in my memory, but I have no idea whether the victim lived or died, nor what happened to the suspects. I rather think they were acquitted and the guilty parties never identified.

Evacuees and administrative staff drew a deep, collective breath of relief as we all settled into a wary peace.

Opposite page: Yakiyasu Uyeoka, soldier of the United States army, stands before the service flag. Each week the number of stars increases as more boys volunteer and are accepted for service. (National Archives)

Call to Arms

One unexpected bonus of the strike
was an improved form of self-government
among the evacuees.

The elective group based on block representation without regard to citizenship had proved to be an efficient way to run a strike and was adapted now to run the truce.

The *issei* returned to leadership roles. More points of view were heard. The general trend was toward a less contentious community, with the majority pulling together instead of finding grounds for continuous disagreement.

But another crisis was in the making.

Immediately after Pearl Harbor and in the effort to avert mass evacuation, the Japanese American Citizens League (JACL), particularly its national president and spokesman, Mike Masaoka, proposed and continued to promote a volunteer combat unit that would demonstrate their total loyalty to the country of their birth. The Federal authorities ignored the idea.

While the *nisei* in Relocation Centers were ineligible to enlist, the very sensitive Military Intelligence checked records to identify Japanese-Americans who could help the U.S. war effort. Not surprisingly, the group most eligible were the *kibei*, those schooled in Japan and most suspect to the FBI. Many of these "iffy" *kibei*, plus some *nisei*, were investigated, cleared, and sent to Minnesota for training. They did magnificent work, translating and breaking the codes of Japan's military. Later under battle conditions, they listened to communications between Japanese pilots and the airfields, and interrogated captured prisoners.

Between December 7, 1941, and Executive Order 9066 to clear the West Coast in February 1942, the FBI, Naval Intelligence, and others in a position to assess the situation saw no threat from any alien or Japanese citizen left on the West Coast. All those considered even remotely suspicious had been interned in the interests of national security.

As far as the investigative groups were concerned, there was no reason for Japanese-Americans already in the military before Pearl Harbor to be discharged, but they were. New volunteers could have been checked on an individual basis, as could any city or state employee or anyone in defense industries. Unfortunately, the propaganda machine moved faster than the Federal experts.

In the months after Pearl Harbor, U.S. military authorities were impressed by the courageous fighting performance of the Japanese enemy forces. Perhaps their U.S. cousins might do the same. They were further impressed with the determined dedication of the young *nisei* in Hawai'i who served wherever they could. Eventually, former National Guard members in Hawai'i were sent to Schofield Barracks to become the Hawaiian Provisional Infantry Battalion, which later became the 100th Infantry Battalion.

Within a year of the outbreak of war, the War Department decided that a Japanese-American volunteer unit would be a great idea, and the announcement to this effect was made on January 28, 1943. At the same time, the WRA was anxious to speed up the leave clearance process so that more evacuees could relocate out of camp, eastward to the Middle West and the East Coast.

Evacuation had occurred in such a hurry that there was no systematic effort to check out individual "loyalty." So, wouldn't it be convenient to have a mass registration? This would provide volunteer recruits and, at last, separate the "loyal" from the "disloyal" for relocation purposes.

In a matter of weeks, the War Department and the WRA joined forces. They rushed through a lengthy form, fated to be misunderstood and poorly received, administered to everyone over the age of 17 in each of the 10 relocation camps.

The form was mistakenly entitled "Application for Leave Clearance," which alarmed the older *issei*. They were beginning to believe that Japan might ultimately be defeated. Whatever their attitude toward the war, the *issei* had taken a position of neutrality, expecting to remain in camps for the duration, and they were making a deliberate effort to get along as peacefully as possible. Faced with this form, the *issei* feared they would be forced to return to their West Coast homes, where people would not welcome back any "Jap."

After the strike, the Poston evacuees were not prepared for this divisive registration. The *nisei*, even though citizens, were not in any mood to volunteer for a segregated military unit. Nor were they prepared to leave their families who seemingly would be ousted from camp. What would their families do without jobs, without money, in California or the unknown world of the eastern states?

Most of the questions on the form concerned birthplace, education, and so forth, but the two final questions caused a furor:

Question 27: Are you willing to serve in the armed forces of the United States on combat duty, wherever ordered?

All *nisei* age 17 and over had to answer this question. The *issei* parents resented the question, wondering why their children should be asked to serve a country that had incarcerated them and taken away all their rights of citizenship. The *nisei* women found the question irrelevant; they had no intention of serving in the military.

Question 28: Will you swear unqualified allegiance to the United States of America and faithfully defend the United States from any or all attack by foreign or domestic forces, *and forswear any form of allegiance or obedience to the Japanese emperor, or any other foreign government, power or organization?*

For the *issei*, this was an impossible question. Their only citizenship was Japanese because the United States would not allow them to become naturalized citizens. How could they forswear allegiance to Japan?

Eventually Question 28 for the *issei* was changed to read, "Will you swear to abide by the laws of the United States and to take no action which would in any way interfere with the war effort of the United States?" However, the rephrasing came too late to undo the serious harm that had been done.

For the *nisei*, Question 27 was the higher hurdle. Many could swear allegiance but were not prepared to serve in the armed forces as long as their parents were in camp. Did it make sense to expect them to volunteer for service in the Pacific where a sentry or a scout could be mistaken for an enemy? But would refusing make them draft dodgers? What were the penalties?

In Hawai'i, there had been no relocation of Japanese or Japanese-Americans, except for those interned by the FBI. There was no registration form administered. Ten thousand young *nisei* volunteered. Nearly 3,000 sailed from Hawai'i for training at Camp Shelby, Mississippi. From the ten Relocation Centers across the U.S., fewer than 1,200 evacuees joined up; the Army had expected 3,500.

In the camps, the *nisei* had three choices on the form:

YES–YES which meant volunteering for the army and swearing allegiance to the U.S. A sure way to be unpopular among their dissident neighbors.

NO–YES which meant they would not volunteer but were loyal to the U.S. Instant label of draft dodger and less than praise from the disaffected.

NO–NO which put them in the disloyal category. Possible peace in some families and among embittered friends.

Volunteers faced ridicule as being suckers for their willingness to serve in a segregated unit (dubbed Jap Crow) under all-Caucasian officers. In the face of expected distrust and racial prejudice, it was no easy decision to leave behind impoverished, emotionally battered parents. If their families had to leave camp, where would they go? How could they survive? Those who had already relocated had settled in cities. Families who came from farms had no urban skills. The army volunteer would earn little more than the $16 or $19 he received in camp, so he wouldn't be able to help his family financially.

Impossible decisions.

Unwilling Bystanders

In February 1943, my roommate, Fran, and I were among the administrative crew asked to assist in the Registration.

Above: A Nisei soldier in uniform visits his family. (National Archives)

Our "briefing" was minimal. We were told: Be sure all questions are answered. Use an interpreter when necessary. Do not hold up the line.

Two Army recruiters stood by when any American-born eligible man—*nisei* or *kibei*—answered Question 27 (enlisting) and 28 (swearing allegiance). The Army recruiters were indifferent at best, brusque and rude at worst.

After barely five months in Poston, we didn't know many of the tired and fearful hundreds who lined up. These people had stood in too many degrading lines already—in Assembly Centers, for barracks assignments, for meals. None of the WRA helpers could do much to lessen the strain, although we did try to explain to the evacuees that the form was not a threat of instant eviction from Poston. Few believed us.

Now and then I saw a familiar face. Goro was only 15, but he came along with his family. He'd been in one of my ninth-grade classes—a quiet, respectful boy, an absolute demon on the baseball diamond. His *issei* father and older *kibei* brother were firm in their NO–NOs. Goro stood by, his head down, unable to look at me. Heartsick, I watched the family move away.

Kobe, a fellow teacher, answered NO–YES under the disapproving eye of the Army recruiter. Kobe later volunteered in the summer of 1943, when the school term ended. He served in the Vosges section of France with the legendary 442nd Regimental Combat Team.

Most of the eligible Poston *nisei* answered the same way—NO to serving in the armed forces and YES to swearing loyalty to the U.S., not at all what the War Department had intended! Others, like Kobe, eventually volunteered to serve.

I asked myself: If I were the eldest son or the only son, would I volunteer?

After the Registration had been completed, all of the NO–NOs were interviewed individually and given the chance to change their answers. None did. Later, key administrative staff from every center went to Washington to serve on a final review board. The Poston Camp I high school principal was typical among that group. He testified to the loyalty of many Poston evacuees, knowing why they answered as they did.

Saburo's father had lost his small hotel and all his hope; Kats' widowed mother was too frail to live alone and yearned to take her husband's ashes back to Japan for burial; Jim's father was interned in New Mexico and his older *kibei* brother was now making decisions for the family; the whole Nakatani family was distraught—the mother remained institutionalized in California with tuberculosis, the youngest daughter had just died from a burst appendix and the older daughter miscarried her first child—so the father and four brothers could not think clearly about their future. Such information probably survives in the archives, but the answers remained as originally given.

For those who answered YES–YES, or NO–YES and volunteered later, their troubles were not over. As volunteers from Poston and other Relocation Centers arrived at Camp Shelby, Mississippi, they faced a totally unexpected problem. The Go-For-Broke volunteers from Hawai'i, where no mass evacuation had occurred, proved instantly antagonistic. The pidgin-speaking "Buddhaheads" from Hawai'i resented these later arrivals who spoke "fancy" English and dubbed them "kotonks," a term allegedly reflecting the sound of their heads when hit. There were many fisticuffs and verbal confrontations. Peace was declared after some of the gung-ho guys from Hawai'i visited Rohwer and Jerome, the two Relocation Centers in Arkansas, where the parents of their fellow soldiers were incarcerated. The Hawai'i *nisei* were shocked at camp conditions and wondered if they themselves would have volunteered from behind the barbed wire fences of Relocation Centers.

Pidgin later served the Buddhaheads well in the foggy Vosges mountains. The nearby Germans couldn't figure out crazy messages such as, "Eh, brah, send gun boltsu chop chop. And ammo kudasai."
Go figure.

Opposite page: Residents of Colorado River Relocation Center for persons of Japanese ancestry requesting repatriation to Japan. (National Archives)

Further Segregation

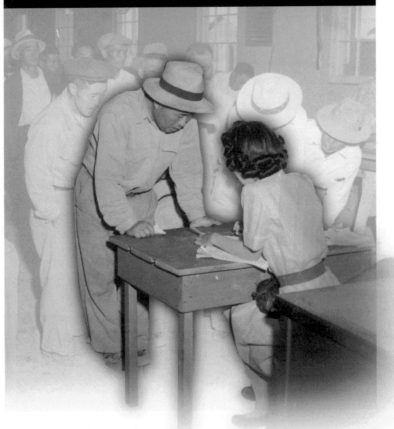

The families had argued and agonized
and finally said YES–YES or NO–NO,
or whatever combination each person chose.

In a matter of days, the Registration was done.

Before the Registration, about 2,800 in all ten camps had requested repatriation to Japan for various reasons. Some had always intended to return to their fatherland. For others, evacuation wiped out any possibility of starting over again in the United States. Those with relatives or property in Japan hoped to start again there. Registration pushed many more older *issei* to file for repatriation and to request expatriation papers for their American-born children, many of them still minors.

Ultimately nearly 4,724 evacuees actually returned to Japan. Of these, 1,658 were *issei*, Japanese returning to their native country—taking with them 1,949 *nisei* minor children who were U.S. citizens. The rest, mostly *kibei*, renounced their U.S. citizenship.

In Congress, the House Un-American Activities Committee was infuriated when they heard about the NO–NOs and wanted the WRA to stop all relocation out of camps, by any evacuees. The State of California instituted seizure actions on evacuee-held land and campaigned to prevent the return of any evacuees after the war.

Those who had answered NO–NO were to be transferred to a segregation center. Tule Lake Relocation Center in California was the camp selected for the purpose. The Tule Lake evacuees who'd said YES–YES would be distributed among the other nine camps. Unfortunately, many of the Tuleans did not want to move. Therefore, Tule Lake ended up with a mixture of about one-third old Tuleans, one-third "segregants," and one-third underage or elderly family members. This proved to be an explosive mix and was badly, even tragically, mishandled. Along with the overcrowding, miscalculation and mismanagement filled that sorriest chapter in the whole sad tale of relocation.

The transferring of evacuees out of Tule Lake and from other centers into Tule Lake was completed in the fall of 1943.

The evacuees in Poston, like those in Tule Lake, had become loath to move, digging in for the duration. Even though there was now an efficient network of church groups, hostels, and committed individuals outside the camps to insure safety, housing, and a welcoming atmosphere in such cities as Chicago, Denver, Minneapolis, Cincinnati, and many smaller communities, many evacuees chose to cling to the security of the known, rather than to risk an unknown world. This attitude deepened as time went by. In the face of this inertia, the WRA encouraged, even pushed, the *nisei* and their families to move out and go eastward.

In 1944, Seabrook Farms, a large producer of frozen vegetables in New Jersey, began recruiting families with an agricultural background. Some 2,500 evacuees went there from the centers. The working conditions were far from ideal, with low pay. But, psychologically, it was better than camp life. And, since these families had received leave clearance, they were free to change jobs if they so chose. By January 1945, 42,600 evacuees had relocated eastward.

However, in spite of the emphasis on relocation, most evacuees remained in the centers until the war was over.

Learning By Doing

The U.S.-born *nisei* students
were the first to respond
to the pressure to relocate.

Above: Evacuee clerk obtaining personal data. (National Archives)

94

I didn't have to prod my Quaker alma mater, Swarthmore, to welcome evacuees as students; the college president was the head of the National Japanese American Student Relocation Council, which ultimately placed some 4,300 students in 500 institutions across the nation; this, in spite of the fact that many large colleges and universities had military contracts and so were closed to evacuees. Another family-connected college, Berea College in Kentucky, founded by my great-grandfather, offered both a welcome and financial help in the form of scholarships and work for board and room. If these young "missionaries" accomplished nothing else, they served to show many Americans from Berea to Chicago, from Peoria to Pittsburgh that Japanese-Americans were indeed Americans and spoke English, yet!

In connection with such relocation, odd assignments came my way in the evenings. I participated in frequent meetings about the "etiquette" of train travel. As though I were an authority! Surprisingly, I knew more than I thought I did.

What should they wear? The evacuees had arrived in Poston wearing summer clothes, adding sweaters or jackets as needed when the temperature dropped. Now, heading to the Midwest and East Coast, more adequate warm clothes were necessary. Thanks to Sears and Montgomery Ward catalogs and a small clothes allowance, they ordered slacks and woolen coats.

Should they brave the dining car? No, they probably couldn't afford it on the $25 cash travel allowance they received. As the war went on, the lines were longer than the dining car could handle. My advice: Whenever the train made a long stop, get off quickly and buy some food from a station vendor, hope that the sandwiches would not be too stale, and further hope that the vendors would assume they were Chinese.

Money, of course, presented a severe problem. But in our small Administration community, when a student was leaving on the night train, we could usually collect some warm clothes and cold cash to ease the parting. The administrative staff could usually spare a sweater or a jacket or a pair of wool socks. However, we could not protect them as they crossed the continent into what was, for them, truly foreign territory.

I knew the old joke that hogs could go nonstop through Chicago but people had to change trains. The trains from the west came into a station from which no east or north or south-bound train left. Those trains left from at least four other railroad stations. As far as I know, it's still true.

The trains from the west usually arrived in the morning, and trains departing in other directions left in the afternoon or evening—a mixed blessing. The travelers had a chance to ask questions, check schedules, find a place to store baggage, and eat a meal. But what do you do with two hours, or ten, in a strange city and you have an Oriental face during a war with Japan? Alerted by telegram, church groups or relatives or people like my parents filled the vacuum by offering food, shelter, and even a bath. Kiyo's leave clearance came through in the fall of 1942. In the flurry of departure, she had little time to assemble a wardrobe. She stayed a couple of days in Chicago, where my mother opened my closet door and let her to take whatever she needed. In the meantime, my father charted her trip to an obscure college in Michigan.

We worked as fast as we could, but not always fast enough. Any individual who left camp, whether for seasonal agricultural work or the Army or college, had to receive leave clearance from the Department of Justice. This clearance was based on information the camp provided about age, education, family background, and staff judgments of ability and "loyalty." The paperwork for such a routine check was often maddeningly slow.

College students with a waiting scholarship didn't always get their high school or college transcripts and leave clearance in time. Yuki was one who missed the start of the fall semester of her freshman year and her chance at a dormitory room. A family traded her a room for some cleaning and baby-sitting. She was grateful, but remembers her first year as a never-ending, catch-up struggle. Men received job offers, but, by the time they received their clearance and lined up housing, the job had long since been filled. Tosh's job in Minneapolis went to someone else, and it was four months before he had another offer.

In March of 1943, I took pen in hand to write my very first protest letter to an editor. *The Ladies Home Journal* had recently published a complete novel which implied that Fifth Column activities were a common problem in Honolulu before Pearl Harbor. In response to my published letter, the editor's note read as follows:

[P]robably not until after the war shall we know for certain whether Pearl Harbor can be blamed entirely on Army and Navy unpreparedness and official Japanese treachery—or whether there were some Jap Fifth Columnists on Oahu."
Well, I tried.

After ten months, I returned to Chicago to keep peace in the family. My mother was not reconciled to the notion that her two daughters would work for their livelihood. If we must be employed, she remained convinced that we should start closer to the top, not at the bottom.

While I stayed with my parents, I enrolled in the University of Chicago summer school, taking courses that I hoped would help me return to the classroom better qualified.

I wasn't sorry to miss the 120-degree Arizona summer heat, but the stalwart staff who stayed told me what I had missed: the desert ablaze with spectacular crimson pigweed, and the bureaucratic drudgery of readying for the eviction of the NO–NOs to Tule Lake and the reception of YES–YESes into Poston.

After an absence of two months, I returned in the fall of 1943 to Camp II, which was half the size of Camp I. During the first year, many staff men had come alone because there was not adequate housing for families. Now more administrative families had arrived and were living in small cottages where they could housekeep.

The mess hall group was, therefore, smaller, made up mostly of single employees. I had a new roommate, Joan, dainty and serious-minded, but good company. She earned the respect and love of her students. She was held in high esteem by the *issei* adults in her evening English classes. I tried her patience by acquiring a roaming, sharp-clawed kitten called Marmalade. Fortunately, our friendship outlasted the feline.

Roommate Joan, our friend Bob W., and I formed a somewhat subversive clique in the regular faculty meetings. I don't recall what the fussing was about, but I sat near and sided with them, seldom speaking, but nodding my head vigorously in agreement with whatever cause they took up.

All of the administrative staff, of course, were free to go at any time outside working hours to Parker if we had a car, and gas for it, or if we could hitch a ride with a friend. Although hardly more than a short escape, such a trip could prove catastrophic. Not all the bad things happened to the evacuees. One Saturday evening, the Camp II school principal and his family went to town. The children, a 12-year-old daughter and an 8-year-old son, went to the movies while their parents bought groceries and other necessaries. In the few minutes after the movie ended and before the parents arrived, an M.P. drove up in a jeep and persuaded the girl to go for a ride, which ended in rape. To my knowledge, the man was never apprehended.

In Camp II, I had the pleasure of a proper tenth-grade classroom. The new school buildings were well designed and well built. The adobe structures were cooler in the warm months, and a fine stove made the rooms cozy on winter mornings when the water in the irrigation ditches froze over. I faced my class of 25 with a modicum of confidence.

One of my students taught me a lesson that I've never forgotten. Haruo was my stove starter and did his work dependably, but he wasn't as conscientious about homework and was mischief incarnate in class. One day, for a now-forgotten offense, I sent him to the principal's office. The principal did everything right. He called the parents and he included me in the meeting after class. The principal was fair, but stern. As the session dragged on with Haruo's mother in tears, his father visibly upset but silent, and Haruo himself mute, I sincerely regretted the misery I had caused.

I learned from that painful experience that teaching belonged in the classroom and discipline was between the student and teacher, not with the principal and students' parents. Poston parents hardly needed a summons from the school just because their high-spirited son had bubbled over. That was the only time I sent a student to be disciplined by the principal.

Just as I began to gain confidence in the classroom, family illness called me back to Chicago.

Above: Two views of new adobe school buildings. (National Archives)

Friends gave me a fine send-off in our favorite Parker bar. From Ma's Diner next door came hot bowls of chili, which we ate while the jukebox played sad cowboy songs. As train-departure time approached, the bar owner presented me with a pint of whiskey—a gift of gold in those wartime days of rationing.

It was a strange and lonesome train trip home over Christmas. Even though it was the height of the war—December 1943—the train was mostly empty. I left behind people who mattered to me, people I wanted to help in whatever small way I could. I also left new friends and, most personally, a man who mattered more than I'd realized. I cried my way past the miles of prairie. I did not know when, if ever, I would see any of these people again.

Above: New Years Fair marble champ. Jerry Osumi, age 11. Opposite page: Nursery school children singing "Twinkle, Twinkle, Little Star." (National Archives)

Time Marched On

The policy-makers' push for evacuees to relocate eastward resulted in the departure of evacuee teachers as they left the camps to continue their education or careers outside.

Consequently, some classes were left without teachers. On the other hand, when whole families were relocated east, the number of students dwindled. For the Director of Education and the school principals, there was never a perfect balance, but they kept on juggling as best as they could.

The hospital and administrative offices, the hog farm and camouflage net factory also lost evacuees to relocation. By mid-1944, 20,000 evacuees had received clearance to leave relocation camps indefinitely, including those who enlisted in the Army.

For some school-age children who spent the whole time in one center, it may have seemed a settled, bearable, even enjoyable period, with friends and sports, and free time. For the decision-makers—parents, young adults, older *issei*, administrative personnel—the period often seemed like one crisis after another—evacuation itself, the strike, registration and resultant segregation.

The older *issei* who remained in camp settled into passive acceptance of camp as an interlude, outside of real life. They felt no pressure to assimilate, no need to be always careful of speech and behavior. The war dragged on and, in spite of some Allied victories, it seemed likely to continue into the distant future. By January 1945, those still in camp expected to stay for an indefinite "duration."

They were in for a surprise.

The Supreme Court ruled on December 31, 1944, that it was illegal to hold a U.S. citizen without filing charges or providing a fair trial. With the war still raging on all fronts, the Departments of Justice, War and Interior (of which War Relocation was then a part) came to a decision: As of January 1945, all "cleared" evacuees could return to the West Coast. This officially rescinded the evacuation authorized by President Roosevelt's Executive Order 9066.

The WRA further announced that the Relocation Centers (except for the Tule Lake Segregation Center) would close within six to nine months. Camp schools would close in June and school records would be sent to Washington, D.C.

On January 24, 1945, the Director of Education in Poston put a good face on the plight of the evacuees by stating his sincere belief concerning the school children:

"We have watched with anxiety the bad effects of life in the relocation center upon their work habits, their behavior, their respect for property, their social attitudes, and their knowledge of the world outside of Poston...[W]e welcome the closing of the schools, the closing of the centers and the return of our young people to the schools of American communities where they belong."

Some 80,000 of the original evacuees remained in camps. Almost all of those in Poston had come from California, mostly from the Los Angeles area. They were stunned. The Los Angeles newspapers made it clear that no Japanese would be welcome. Who would dare to return? And, after three years in camp with no home to return to, where would the evacuees go? Fearing for their own safety, the evacuees were convinced that the U.S. Government, having incarcerated them, was obligated to maintain the centers until the war ended.

The administrative staff was also shocked by the Federal decision. Job applications were quickly mailed off. Understandably, those who received job offers accepted them and left camp. Given the school calendar, most of the teachers remained and a few stayed into autumn to help with the "mopping up."

In spite of all the uncertainties, V-E (Victory in Europe) Day in May 1945 marked a day of triumph for the Allies and a relief for families with sons in the 442nd and other units in Europe.

In mid-July, the first atomic bomb had been tested in New Mexico, mysteriously lighting up the sky for hundreds of miles in all directions, even as far away as Poston on the western boundary of Arizona. The country knew nothing of this powerful new weapon. On August 6 (Japan time), one of these bombs was dropped on Hiroshima and a second one, on Nagasaki three days later, killing nearly a quarter of a million people and maiming thousands more. Within a week, Japan surrendered.

Although few of us were immediately aware of the nuclear devastation, we recognized that this bomb was different and could change the world. For American Japanese, even with limited information, the destruction had diluted the joy of victory.

In Hawai'i, particularly, there was great concern because many of the *issei* had emigrated from Hiroshima prefecture. In addition to relatives left behind, there were sons and daughters who'd been visiting and were caught there when war broke out.

Therefore, V-J Day in August was very different, coming after the atomic bombing of Hiroshima and Nagasaki. Worry and sorrow overrode jubilation. For the *issei*, Japan was, after all, their homeland; the *nisei* had cousins there. Even if they'd never met their relatives, they couldn't rejoice at such a devastating end to the war.

For the 4,700 repatriates/expatriates who had answered NO–NO on the Army Registration form in 1943 or had requested repatriation even before that, there was little cause to rejoice. Those who had reached Japan during the war were not welcomed into a country at war, suffering from shortages of even the bare necessities. Those who arrived at war's end faced hardships that may have made Relocation Centers look good. They were housed in sheds near the docks, dependent for food and care upon the Occupation Forces who had to cope with a whole devastated nation.

In June 1946, the War Relocation Authority officially ceased to exist. All records were transferred to the U.S. Archives, where scholars continue to study and analyze reams of statistics. While scholars can chronicle a great deal in numbers—how many people and how many dollars—they often miss the human dimensions of an unnecessary government action. This sad chapter in American history cannot be told in figures alone. As citizens of the U.S., we must recognize that this mass evacuation resulted in the dislocation of 110,000 lives, the physical hardships of camp life, prolonged uncertainty about the future, and feelings of helplessness and defeat.

Sometime in my past

    At Pearl Harbor my ancestors and I became enemies.

    The deaf hear me shout that I was I and

    Not my ancestor-enemy, but which was which was hard to

    Tell; we surely looked alike.

Sometime in my past

    I chose America but America rejected me,

    Banished from view my foe-tinged face.

    At gunpoint I and those I resembled went to concentrate,

    We took of our belongings only what we could carry.

    Into ten sentry-guarded camps 110,000 of us were

    Encircled by barbed wire and were

    Concentrated.

    Searchlights raked our dignity.

Sometime in my past

    Home was a 25 x 25 foot, unpartitioned space for me,

    My parents and stranger-bachelor (minimum four bodies

    To a cubicle); straw-stuffed pallets our beds.

    Meals in the mess hall and a communal washhouse we

    Shared with two hundred others in our block.

    More than three years I "gave" to my nation's war effort

    As voluntary exile, a choice I created

    When in truth I had none.

• • •

—Excerpted from *Passionate Rage* by Noriko Sawada Bridges Flynn

A Deserted Camp

During 1944 and most of 1945,
while the evacuees and administrative staff
in Poston and other relocation centers were
struggling with efforts to increase relocation
out of camp and maintaining services within
each center, I was in and around Chicago,
dependent on occasional letters from Poston
friends to keep me informed.

I was working on a master's degree in education at the suburban Winnetka Graduate Teachers College. There, I finally had a chance at practice teaching, for about six weeks. When Mr. J., my overseeing teacher, went into the Navy, I inherited two senior English classes and directed the senior play. I was lucky; the students in that suburban school were all smart, college-bound, and highly motivated. The following fall of 1944 in Chicago, I had my own ninth-grade homeroom and taught English and Social Studies. Two summers of subject-matter courses and a year and a half of night classes in the necessary teacher-training courses had finally given me a measure of confidence previously lacking. In the fall of 1945, I earned my sheepskin and never entered a classroom again.

More importantly, the man-I-left-behind came east from Poston. After a modest wedding, we returned to camp in early November 1945, so my husband, as Director of Education, could finish up his paperwork and final report on the Poston schools. Officially the camp had ceased to be. All evacuees had left by car or train. Any evacuee who hadn't selected a destination was sent back to his community of origin. We looked out over the deserted camp on a cold November night and saw a single lonely light in a far barracks. Another night, another light. Each time, a staff member would investigate and, each time, he found a solitary evacuee man in a bare room. The man was put on the next train back to California for a future unknown. These were forlorn *issei* bachelors, without family, with no place else to go. Some returned to Poston as often as three times.

I was back on the payroll to finish the clerical work—sorting school materials, preparing transcripts to be filed with the U.S. Office of Education, and finishing up final reports. I sat in front of a very long-carriage typewriter to copy off statistics, original and carbons. The official record of every single individual in each of the ten Relocation Centers included 31 items from name through height and weight to religion. This mountain of paperwork now rests in the National Archives.

Opposite page: This shade built as a protection from the heat of the sun has already served its purpose, as have the home-made chairs and benches. (National Archives)

Our apartment in the new family quarters, Rainbow Village, was quite a treat compared to the old barracks. A proper kitchen was a mixed blessing. During my brief period of independent living in 1944–45, I had learned to boil rice, cream dried beef, and stuff peppers. Not a balanced menu for every day, but we muddled through. And, of course, I had married a man of many talents, including cookery. I discovered his culinary ability on New Year's Day. A sociable woman, who shared the typing chores with me, hosted a fine Eve party where we overcelebrated. We'd bought a "New York dressed" chicken. The feathers were off. Period. In the morning I took one look at it and went back to bed. No problem for my new husband. He understood fowl anatomy and coped with great dispatch. I really enjoyed the results.

Cooking was not the only challenge. In the early Poston days, with seersucker and easy-iron chambray, I'd struggled through the laundry. But at the advanced age of 25, I particularly didn't know about seven shirts a week. Curiously, I cannot remember the Saturday morning process of washing clothes. And what about sheets and towels? I can remember tubs in the laundry building and clotheslines, so we probably had no modern appliances. The clothes dried quickly in the desert air. But I do remember the ironing! After two months' practice, I finally reduced my ironing time to a half hour per shirt.

My learning didn't stop with shirts. Having grown up in a non-sports family, I didn't realize that some men listened to ball games on Saturday afternoon. The radio accompanied my efforts at the ironing board. By the end of the afternoon, I was usually quite testy.

In January of 1946, we parted with the last of the administrative staff, drove away from Poston with hardly a backward look at the empty barracks, the deserted community, the scene of shameful injustice.

Opposite page: Survivors of the Lost Battalion presented this silver plaque to their Nisei rescuers. (442nd Archives and Learning Center)

Most Went West

To the
442nd INFANTRY REGIMENT
With Deep Sincerity And Upmost Appreciation
For the Gallant Fight To Effect Our Rescue
After We Had Been Isolated For Seven Days.

1st Bn., 141st INFANTRY REGIMENT

Biffontaine, France
From 24th To 30th October
1944

Virtually all of those remaining
in relocation centers chose to return
to the West Coast.

The evacuees who returned to find their land, buildings, and equipment intact were the lucky ones. Their communities may not have rolled out a red carpet, but the evacuees experienced less antagonism than expected. Only about 30 incidents of violence were reported—stores or barns burned, occasional shots fired, and cars cruising by. But news of such incidents traveled widely.

The unfortunate ones—and they were many—returned to houses that had been taken over by neighbors and to farms that had been left untended. Orchards had withered from lack of care, and greenhouses had been shattered. Even their possessions in government warehouses had been stolen or neglected to the point of uselessness due to careless storage, rain damage, or vandalism—fragile Satsuma ware broken or missing, photograph albums pulled apart, clothing scattered and torn. A Buddhist temple, vacant during the war, had been broken into and vandalized.

In Portland and Seattle, customers boycotted the farm produce grown by returned evacuees and racist signs remained in retail stores: "No Jap Trade Wanted." Obtaining life or fire insurance, as well as business licenses for many activities, remained difficult.

On the bright side, many communities organized welcoming committees to help the evacuees find housing and jobs. Church groups, community leaders, and the newspapers actively urged cooperation and assistance. Individual *hakujin* friends from before the war stood fast by the returning evacuees. Army representatives in various settings praised the *nisei* bravery and their parents' forbearance and dignity. West Coast city and state officials got the message that tolerance and fair play were the rules of the game henceforth.

Housing was the most urgent problem. Many evacuee women sought domestic work in order to find a place to live. Two, three and even four families would rent a single house.

On the job front, many farms, stores, hotels, and restaurants had fallen into other hands. Men who'd lost land leases and personal goods had no money to begin again. Many agricultural workers shifted into cities. The Little Tokyos had been taken over by war workers, so those returning settled into unfamiliar places. Increasing numbers of *nisei* applied for white collar jobs, but did not always find them quickly in state and local government offices. Public schools were slow to hire evacuees during the first few postwar years. For the first time, Japanese names appeared on the welfare rolls.

Those who returned to farming favored flowers and landscaping over orchards or truck gardening. Few went back to fishing. The *issei* were mostly too old; few *nisei* had the necessary skills, although some did go into the fish canneries.

The veterans, of course, benefited from the G.I. bill. Reports of their heroic deeds in Europe had preceded their return. Nevertheless, some local American Legion posts behaved like racists. Most notoriously, in Hood River, Oregon, Post 22 voted to remove the names of 16 *nisei* inscribed on a commemorative plaque, including ten who had been awarded the Purple Heart. The national headquarters disapproved and directed the Post to reinstate the names, which it did—grudgingly.

Across the Atlantic, *nisei* soldiers had been among the first to reach Dachau, the infamous concentration camp in Germany. These liberators had not known of the slave labor and death camps and were totally unprepared for the horrors they saw: the emaciated prisoners, starving and bewildered, who probably would not have survived even a few days more. The prisoners had never seen Japanese faces before and feared that the Asian arm of the Axis had arrived to kill them.

The veterans aren't always forthcoming about their war experiences, whether at Monte Cassini or the Vosges mountains. But in interviews after a 50th commemoration in Bruyeres, France, reported in *The Honolulu Advertiser* in October 1944, several admitted to bittersweet memories. Masu, for one, had lost friends in the do-or-die rescue of the "Lost Battalion" when his unit suffered 800 casualties in order to save 200 in the daring and successful rescue. When Masu returned to France to meet the survivors, he heard of the elderly French lady who'd said in advance, "I hope the little men come back. They truly saved us."

Only recently have the survivors of the Military Intelligence Service, recruited out of relocation centers, been recognized for their deeds. Their military records as noncombatants have finally been declassified; their presence was never publicized during the war. In places such as Iwo Jima and Okinawa, they risked their lives trying to "talk" armed Japanese soldiers out of caves, or they interrogated the few captured prisoners. They served in Burma and the Philippines and, after the war, some put their language skills to further use in the occupation of Japan. By war's end, some 33,000 *nisei* had served in various branches of the U.S. military, receiving nearly 5,000 medals, awards, and citations.

Each evacuee has an individual story of return and resettlement, some heartening, some shocking. Time, the glory of the 442nd war record, and community leaders standing firm, most notably, the Japanese—alien and citizen—and continuing to be better than good citizens in order to be equal, have led toward ultimate acceptance and recognition.

Above: Recently freed prisoners from one of the Dachau Work Camps (U.S. Signal Corps.)
(442nd Archives and Learning Center)

We Went East

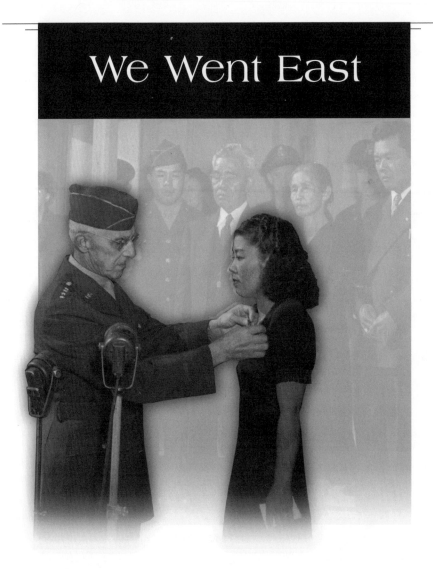

A chapter was closed, but the story was far from finished. Not for me, not for the evacuees, not for the U.S. Government.

My husband and I moved to Washington, D.C., to look for jobs. In those "glory days" of Federal employment, my husband had accumulated months of annual leave. This allowed him lots of time to investigate possible new jobs—South America entailed learning Spanish, Germany had no appeal, and Japan wouldn't accept wives. With his background in school administration, he qualified easily for the U.S. Office of Education, which was concerned with libraries and colleges, as well as elementary and secondary education. He took his time considering all the alternatives.

While he went off to interviews, I sought a temporary job, finding a Grade 3 position as a statistical clerk. In the federal government, Civil Service grades began at 1 and worked up to 18. Grade 3 seemed truly the lowest possible grade, since I've yet to meet a Grade 1 or 2. But it was a bit of cash coming in. I was working with a few friends, since my employer was again the War Relocation Authority in the final six-month close down of the census and other statistical records of the ten Relocation Centers.

Margie had spent the closing months in Poston supervising the tedious task of assembling and typing the camp records. Now she ran the statistical show in Washington.

My immediate boss, Bob, had been an evacuee at the Manzanar Relocation Center. He was a quiet fellow, but patient with my mathematical ignorance. His wife, Minnie, was a *nisei* who'd been caught in Japan on December 7, 1941, while visiting her grandparents. She'd lived with them on their small farm—no plumbing, dirt floors, nothing beyond small stoves to warm the feet but not the room. Even on the farm, food was scarce and the work was hard.

As the war went on and army demands for food increased, rice was mixed half and half with wheat, and meat was rarely available. When leather supplies ran out, the people resorted to wooden clogs instead of shoes. Perhaps Minnie's greatest difficulty was facing the hostility of the villagers. As a "foreigner" from America, she was treated like a spy. Nearly everyone shunned her. Even her elderly grandparents, lifetime

Opposite page: General Joseph Stilwell presents the Distinguished Service Cross to Kazuo Masuda's sister because Army rules prevented him from presenting it to Kazuo's mother because she was an enemy alien. (National Archives)

residents of the community, became suspect by Minnie's very presence. Only after the war could Minnie return to the U.S.

In June 1946, the War Relocation Authority closed down. Several of us lowly clerks transferred to Public Assistance jobs in the Federal Security Agency (later named the Department of Health, Education and Welfare). We kept records of charitable organizations that applied for surplus property released after the war—desks, paper, typewriters, even real estate. The charities had low priority and received little beyond filling lots of forms out.

Margie went to work in the U.S. Department of Agriculture, where she handled super-secret statistics on crop projections. Bob found a non-Government job, while Minnie improved her secretarial skills. As a "foreigner" from Canada in a sensitive job, Margie was forever pursued by the FBI, which couldn't seem to accept her close friendship with the *nisei*. It seemed ridiculous.

In the early 1950s, when Minnie and I worked together in the Children's Bureau, Minnie had applied for a new job and given my name as a reference. The FBI came around to check. The man who interviewed me must have been a new recruit in training. He was young, wide-eyed, and not too bright.

I answered the routine questions: How long had I known her? In what capacity? Was she dependable? Honest? Being prone to gabbiness, I didn't limit myself to monosyllables of "yes" and "excellent." When I dropped some remarks about my husband and me visiting them at their apartment and at our house, his face showed disbelief. "You know them socially!" he gasped. "But, of course," was my obvious response.

By then I had advanced to a Grade 11 and had some clout. I like to think that Minnie got an extra point for knowing us, even though in the 1940s Margie had lost points by knowing the *nisei*. Silly man, silly FBI.

Over the years Minnie and Bob had two beautiful daughters. Then, devastatingly, Bob's lingering fatigue proved to be tuberculosis. The sanitarium costs sapped their finances, as well as Bob's mental outlook. He'd had it with Washington, and they returned to his uncle's farm near Sacramento. For a few years, Minnie sent a message-less card at Christmas. Then, silence. Letters went unanswered and, even though they are still listed in the Sacramento phone book, no one answers at their number. We miss them.

My husband had finally opted for the U.S. Office of Education and, after a succession of rented rooms and dismal apartments, we bought a house in Virginia and settled into 20 years of Federal employment. The buses were "interstate" and integrated, but the movies and every other facility in Virginia and in the District of Columbia were Jim Crow. Our Negro colleagues could not eat in "white" restaurants, try on clothes in department stores, or use public restrooms except in Federal buildings.

Civil servants in Maryland and Virginia could do little politically; the Hatch Act effectively stopped political activities, except inside the voting booth. The District of Columbia was administered by Congress and basically ruled by a committee chairman from the South.

While the *nisei* were in training at Camp Shelby, Mississippi, they had run into segregation and weren't sure whether they were considered "white" or "black," since they were neither.

The neighboring towns accepted them as "white," but they often gave bus drivers a hard time by insisting on sitting in the rear when seats were available or getting into fights with the driver when he wouldn't stop for Negroes along the bus route.

In Washington, D.C., the *nisei* continued to be accepted as "white"; Southerners in the East were not accustomed to Asians and drew no color line against them.

The 442nd Regimental Combat Team returned in 1946. On July 19, while we huddled under umbrellas, President Truman, in belted raincoat and two-tone shoes, presented the unit's seventh Presidential Citation and said:

...You fought not only the enemy, but you fought prejudice—
and you won. Keep up that fight, and we will continue to
win—to make this great republic stand for what the Constitution
says it stands for: "The welfare of all the people all the time."

President Truman's praise contrasted sharply with General Stilwell's presentation of the Distinguished Service Cross for Staff Sgt.

Kazuo Masuda, who was killed while fighting in Italy. An Army rule prohibited the General from presenting the medal to Kazuo's mother because she was an enemy alien. The General pinned the medal on Kazuo's citizen sister, who then pinned it on her mother.

During our years in the Washington area, we kept in touch with a few Poston friends living nearby. George, the bearded Spanish teacher, set up his own Speedy-Q print shop. When Congress needed some extra fast printing, his was one of the chosen few to help out.

Above: On their return home in 1946, veterans of the 442nd Regimental Combat Team were reviewed in Washington by President Harry Truman and other top officials. President Truman salutes the colors before awarding the unit's seventh Presidential Citation (Wide World Photo) (National Archives)

His daughter, on a quick trip to a nearby shopping center, entered her name in a drawing for a swimming pool. To George's dismay, she won. He lost most of his vegetable garden and gained a lot of maintenance, including an expensive fence. His neighbors were delighted, and so were we. We enjoyed an annual swim-in and bounteous feast.

Handsome Hajime, armed with a law degree, settled in the Washington area. He and his classy wife and her mother feted us with an elegant New Year's observance and they graced several of our parties. We saw them each summer beside George's pool before Hajime's import-export legal business and travel kept him away. His life ended abruptly as one of the victims of an airplane bombed by terrorists over Lockerbie, Scotland, in December 1988.

In 1945, Ben, another Poston teacher, returned to California from Poston with failing vision and little optimism. His depression lasted many months. Laboriously he put himself back together and attended the University of California, Berkeley. With a reader and Braille, he graduated and eventually went on to set up and become head of the San Jose Braille Transcription Project, now a national resource center.

He visited D.C. on two occasions, protected only by his white cane. He surmounted two obstacles: the ever-present ethnic prejudice on the West Coast, and the latent suspicion that the blind are incompetent. Interestingly, he remains the truest believer in America as the land of opportunity.

In his late thirties, he married Kimie. She'd had to wait until 1952 before the U.S. Government finally allowed the *issei* to become naturalized American citizens; she was one of the first *issei* in California to become a citizen after the war. In 1998, he published his autobiography.*

*Ben Sanematsu, *Inward Light: An Asian American Journey*, Asian American Curriculum Project, Inc., San Mateo, CA.

Nikki was an on-again, off-again connection. In Poston she had seemed a respectful, even submissive only child. Her parents objected to her relocating, so she remained in camp, working in the office of the Chief Engineer and later in the Relocation Office. After the war, she asserted her independence. Her parents died before she married the most notorious labor leader on the West Coast docks. This surprised and probably shocked the Japanese community. Since California did not allow intermarriage, they eloped, only to find the same prohibition in Nevada. After some fast legal footwork and a U.S. District Court judge, they were able to tie the knot.

We met them in San Francisco some years later. We knew Harry only by his tough "reputation" and were enchanted to watch him play on the floor with his infant daughter, more pussycat than tiger. Some years after Harry died, Nikki married his long-time management counterpart. She has published fine stories and articles, but they don't reflect her quick, sardonic wit.

Taffee rose to the head of the math department at the University of Massachusetts. We saw him occasionally when we visited our Number Three son and family near Boston. When Taffee's daughter Riki showed up in Honolulu in 1976 to be married, we stood in for her parents. We directed her to a doctor for the required premarital exam and soon thereafter found her a minister and a church to be married in. Since neither the bride nor groom knew anyone in Honolulu, we gave them away, served as attendants, and provided the total guest list.

In 1991, Riki and her family returned here for a 20th anniversary celebration. Riki's two children were incredibly patient while we caught up on the intervening years. Riki and her husband "happened by" again in 1997. Ah, to be young again.

Kiyo remains an unseen connection to Poston. Hard to believe we've never met. My image of her is based on 50-year-old descriptions— tiny, gentle, maybe scared. Tiny she may be, possibly gentle, but her life since 1942 does not sound even a little bit scared.

She'd left camp in the fall of 1942, just a name, for whom the Welfare Director was collecting warm clothes and the names of people who might help her along the way. Hers was the first name I telegraphed to my parents in Chicago. They met her train and took her to their apartment and into their hearts. My father checked train schedules to get her to her college destination in Michigan. My mother concentrated on feeding her.

A year later in Camp II, I met her father, who was enrolled and working very hard in my roommate's English class. He was like many others who wanted to learn to write to their children—away in college, out on seasonal agricultural leave and, later, when they served in the Army.

In 1969, when my mother and my husband and I had settled in Honolulu, Kiyo's father took a long-anticipated trip to Japan. On his way home, he looked us up and presented my mother with a delicate Japanese fan. Now that fan decorates our living room wall. Until he died in 1984, he sent gracious Christmas messages to my mother.

Kiyo married a non-Japanese man, probably to her parents' dismay. Her nurse's training in college led her into the Sacramento school system, where she worked as a school nurse. She created and copyrighted the Blackbird Vision Screening System to test very young children, as well as retarded and nonverbal children. This system is now being used nationwide. In 1990 on our way through Sacramento, I finally had a chance to talk to her on the phone, the closest I've ever come to seeing her. At that time she was immersed in all the facets of planning to erect a monument in Poston to commemorate the relocation years.

Two years later, in 1992, when the monument was dedicated, Kiyo and I were both there, but we didn't meet. Kiyo had many friends to meet and greet and too many chores, including checking on a friend who was felled by the heat and taken to the local hospital. I still hope for a future encounter.

Miwa came into my life not from Poston, but from the Topaz Relocation Center in Utah. She'd been studying to be a concert pianist in Tokyo and returned to the U.S., only to be swept away to a Relocation Center. While I was in Chicago working toward my teaching credentials in 1943, she was coming to terms with the end of her musical career. By then, my brother was part of the training program at the University of Chicago, for those who would ultimately be part of the Occupation Forces in Japan.

Miwa moved in with him and his wife and young daughter. With no specified job, she gave the daughter weekly piano lessons. She also typed my brother's manuscript, *The Japanese Nation, A Social Survey,* which was published in paperback as a text for the Armed Forces destined for Japan when the war ended.

At my brother's request, she translated *The Diary of a Japanese Innkeeper's Daughter.*** She was hardly idle, but she looks back on herself then as downright *unhuman.* After nearly two years of restrictions and regimentation in camp, she'd lost confidence, joy, and spontaneity. She never willingly left the Chicago apartment alone. She shut herself off from the world, trusting no one, making no new friends. After six months, she realized she had to face the world again. The world included Columbia University, typing, library work, and ultimately a position as Head of the Japanese Section of the East Asian Library there, a far different career than a concert pianist, but rewarding nonetheless.

In 1995, she journeyed to Japan to be decorated by the Emperor with the Order of the Precious Crown (Wisteria), in recognition of her efforts as a librarian to develop closer relations and understanding between the U.S. and Japan. After surgery on her left hand, she philosophizes about a musical career that never was: "For a librarian to have a hand that can no longer span an octave has no significance whatsoever. Life has been benevolent to me."

These are a few of the people we have kept up with sporadically, by mail or at class reunions. At such reunions, my husband, as the former high school principal of Camp I and then as Director of Education for all three camps, is always summoned to the podium to make a speech. His presence seems to provide a semi-official cast to the proceedings.

**Kai, Miwa, translator. *The Diary of a Japanese Innkeeper's Daughter.* Edited and annotated by Robert J. Smith and Kazuko Smith, Cornell East Asia Papers #36. Cornell University. 1984.

We realize that our friends do not represent all the possible paths that the evacuees have taken since Poston days. We also recognize that those who return to reunions tend to have pleasant memories of their school years. They have succeeded and have enough confidence to face their former classmates. Those whose lives were shattered by the relocation experience have no reason to revive unhappy memories.

"It's been over half a century
since our days of trial in Poston—
a whole lifetime ago
I think often I wouldn't want to go through it,
not for a million dollars,
but I wouldn't want to have missed it either.
It has actually made my life richer and fuller
in words I can't describe."

• • •

—Part of a letter to the author from Sunao Imoto, a Poston teacher

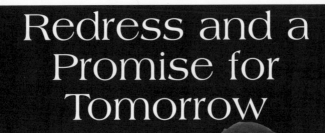

Redress and a Promise for Tomorrow

Can we point with pride to progress?
Yes and no. Under pressure from the Japanese
American Citizens League, determined lawyers, and
other interested groups and individuals, the
Department of Justice reviewed the cases of *issei*
repatriates and bitter *nisei* expatriates who had
turned their backs on the United States.

Above: Mrs. Haru Dairiki of Sacramento, 102 years old, receiving redress check and
government apology from Attorney General Richard Thornburgh at a ceremony in
Washington, D.C., October 9, 1990. Photo by Kevin P. Reilly. (National Japanese
American Historical Society)

The renunciation statute was voided in 1947. Of the 5,766 Japanese Americans who renounced their U.S. citizenship, 4,978 did have their citizenship reinstated

In 1952 the U.S. caught up a little with its democratic principles. The Walter-McCarran Immigration and Naturalization Act made it possible for all Asians to become naturalized citizens. Within a dozen years, some 46,000 *issei* had studied, passed the test, and sworn allegiance. But the Walter-McCarran Act still included wording from the Internal Security Act of 1950 in Title II, which provided for the detention of those who "will engage in, or probably will conspire with others to engage in, acts of espionage or sabotage." Another battle to be fought, and eventually it was won when this section was removed under President Lyndon Johnson in 1965.

The Civil Rights Act of 1964, spearheaded by and for African-Americans, benefited all minorities. At the same time, the Japanese-Americans were seeking their own specific recognition and acceptance. Caucasian lawyers, notably James Purcell and Wayne Collins, petitioned the courts to protest the firing of Japanese-Americans after Pearl Harbor, the curfew, the evacuation, and the renunciation statute. Over the years, many of the individual cases worked their way up to the Supreme Court, with various results.

Above: *Issei* taking oath of citizenship at Hollywood Bowl in the mid-fifties. They were the last of the immigrants to the U.S. to be granted the right to naturalization in 1952. Photo by Toyo Miyatake. © 1978 by Archie Miyatake.

Outside the courts, in 1976, President Gerald Ford made an official announcement that the mass evacuation had been a national mistake, a small step toward righting a serious wrong.

The Japanese American Citizens League, which had been so unpopular with many Japanese for urging cooperation with the government in spite of evacuation, now became a militant force demanding redress. At their 1970 convention, they demanded no less than an official apology from the U.S. Government and $20,000 in cash for each individual placed in a Relocation Center during the war. Not by any means were all of the convention delegates enthusiastic or optimistic, but they went on record anyway.

In 1979, the JACL National Committee for Redress endorsed the creation of a government commission to investigate and recommend appropriate redress. The National Coalition for Redress/Reparations in Los Angeles and the National Council for Japanese American Redress in Seattle placed their emphasis on redress in the form of direct cash payments to the evacuees.

To seek redress, two bills were introduced in Congress in 1979. One of the bills was numbered 442 in honor of the 442nd Regimental Combat Team. The official Commission on Wartime Relocation and Internment of Civilians was established in 1980. The Commission delivered its report, which recommended cash reparations, yet Congress dragged its feet by enacting a bill without appropriating any money. Finally, in 1988, President Ronald Reagan signed the Civil Liberties Act into law, providing $20,000 cash payments to begin in 1990. This seemingly generous allotment was worth about $2,700 in 1945 dollars. The first checks would go to the oldest survivors. Many of the *issei*, who deserved it the most, had died. About 60,000 evacuees were eligible to receive the nontaxable (except in Mississippi, Kansas, and Texas, which demanded a state tax bite) $20,000 each. An official apology was signed and read by President Bush in 1990.

Redress and the token reparations served two important purposes. Firstly, the *issei* could stop internalizing their humiliation and bitterness. What had they done wrong to their adopted country or to their children? For the aging *issei*, the feeling of shame was deeper than reason; they had to know and have others know, officially, that they had done nothing wrong.

Secondly, these *issei* were now willing to talk to their *nisei* children and *sansei* grandchildren about those desolate years in camp. Evacuation had been a nonsubject, never discussed. Now the *issei* could finally express their resentment against a country which made their Japanese background a badge of shame. They could now describe their American experience and the prejudice that had surrounded them. For the first time, the second and third generation learned about relocation from the *issei* point of view—the shock, the helplessness, the financial devastation, the physical and emotional suffering.

Furthermore, the *issei* could now try to convey what Japanese culture was all about, what Japanese values were, and why they were important. Their descendants now have an appreciation that had been lacking before redress became official.

Until World War II, all immigrants aspired to assimilate into the melting pot. In theory, if everyone lived among everyone else without ghettos, all would be well, and a new American would emerge.

The War Relocation Authority effort to relocate evacuees to jobs and colleges in the east and to encourage young *nisei* men to volunteer for the Army—albeit in a segregated unit—seemed to be a great opportunity for assimilation. These young people, who'd never known anything beyond the West Coast, would have the chance to see more of the country and widen their limited horizons. To a great extent, this happened, but World War II brought changing attitudes toward democracy and equality. Now diversity has become the goal and bilingualism an instrument to insure that each ethnic group can preserve its culture.

Minorities have demanded and obtained special ethnic studies in universities and more opportunities in employment. Schools make an effort to extend recognition beyond the Christian teachings, to note the existence of other religions, other customs. And, of course, Martin Luther King, Jr., Day is a national holiday.

Yes, we have come a long way. Does this mean that the American people and our government are approaching color blindness? Hardly. Ask any African-American. Ask Bruce Yamashita, who filed a racial discrimination complaint against the U.S. Marine Corps in 1989, which was not settled in his favor until 1994. Or talk to a Japanese-Peruvian who was removed from Peru and incarcerated in the U.S., with final approval of a $5,000 reparation in 1998.

Could the mass evacuation of a racial group happen again? As we look at the *nisei* and what they have accomplished in business and academia, in the professions and the arts, we can assume that it will not happen to them. They are coming of age politically and stand ready to defend their rights and meet their responsibilities.

Despite Emma Lazarus' words on the Statue of Liberty promising to open our arms to welcome the "tired...poor...huddled masses yearning to breathe free," America has a well-documented, racist, anti-immigrant history.

Immigrant peoples will continue to be at risk as long as American employers exploit cheap labor. Women seeking house cleaners, growers needing seasonal harvesters, garment factory owners wanting sweat-shop employees routinely ignore legal requirements about Social Security, Medicare, minimum wage, and other workers' rights. Now, at the end of the century, there is growing antagonism against immigrants, whether legal or illegal. Seemingly, there are "too many" immigrant groups that stand out in too many communities. Pressure is mounting in the states and in Congress to do something. Affirmative action programs have been wiped out. What next?

A look back at evacuation is a reminder that panic and prejudice carry a high cost in dollars and sense. To relocate 110,000 people, the Army spent some $89 million to set up Assembly Centers, build Relocation Centers, and feed those people until the War Relocation Authority took over. The WRA itself spent $160 million between the spring of 1942 and final closure in the summer of 1946. That $249 million was money ill-spent.

The property losses to the Japanese were estimated by the Federal Reserve Bank at $400 million—a far cry from the meager reparation payments in 1990. Settlement under the Evacuation Claims Act continued for 17 years, with barely $132 million recouped. Few evacuees had written proof of the value of an old tractor or a new refrigerator that had been grabbed up in a quick sale for a few dollars. Examiners had no idea of the worth of a *bonsai* plant or an antique scroll of calligraphy. The claims applied only to tangible real or personal property, not to the intangibles of sentiment or business relationships established over the decades. Lawyers' fees ate up about 10 percent. Most of the evacuees who tried to obtain compensation settled for much less, about 10 cents regained for each dollar lost.

At a time of a severe manpower and food shortage, the nation lost the industry of Japanese farmers and fishermen, the productivity of people who might have served in all manner of jobs, and the taxes these relocated people would have paid! Beyond the dollar cost to evacuate 110,000 people, the social cost of uprooting an entire racial minority, two-thirds of whom were citizens, is incalculable.

Americans should not forget that we all come of immigrant stock. Even Native Americans came from Asia, Hawaiians from the South Pacific, and African-Americans, under duress, were brought in from Africa. But now some are beginning to wonder if a country of such differing peoples and cultures can remain one nation. Will ethnic diversity lead to fragmentation?

Are we a melting pot or a kaleidoscope? Do we blend together indistinguishably, or do we stand out and shine as parts of a greater whole? The homogeneity of drab burlap or the richness of silk brocade? America has a choice to make—in school, at the ballot box, in church or the workplace, in every facet of daily life.

• • •

At the February 1985 Poston Homecoming, a reunion of Poston Community Baptists, a black minister remarked:

"...I've been thinking and I believe what makes the Japanese-American different from other American minorities is that they are able to let go of their bitterness, and because they didn't have that to hold them back, they were able to progress and achieve all the great things that they have."
—Quoted in the March 8, 1985 issue of the *Pacific Citizen*

Finale

On October 6, 1992,
nearly 2,000 people revisited Poston,
coming from as far away as Japan.

Above: Poston Memorial Monument. Frank and Joanne Iritani, *Ten Visits: Accounts of Visits to all The Japanese American Relocation Centers*, Japanese American Curriculum Project. ©1995 by Frank and Joanne Iritani.

The temperature soared to 109 degrees under a cloudless, sunny sky in Arizona. Many of us there for the first time in 50 years had forgotten how hot an October day could be. A few came well prepared with blue plastic canopies; some brought umbrellas or parasols. Others were lucky to have a cap or dark glasses. We blessed the planners who gave everyone a souvenir fan. Six people were felled by the heat, including a girl in the local high school band and a man who'd traveled by bus with us from California.

In 1942, most of the arable Indian land was leased out to local white farmers, so Poston's three camps had taken over the arid acres. The Mohave Indians visible in the town of Parker in 1942–45 appeared to be unemployed and indolent. The Parkerites seemed to like the Indians as little as they liked the "Japs."

As we drove toward the town of Parker these many years later and turned south to Poston, we hardly recognized the terrain. Instead of blowing dust and grayed mesquite trees, we saw alfalfa and cotton growing lushly green in every direction, all carefully tilled by the Indians. Parker had left behind its one-horse image. Now it promoted the area itself as a vacation resort with something for everyone—boat racing and other water sports on the Colorado River, golf and horseback riding, off-road racing and rock gathering, and deluxe motels!

The three Poston camps had ceased to exist.

We were assembled to dedicate the Poston Memorial Monument. The Tribal Council of the Colorado River Indian Tribes (Mohave, Chemehuevi, Hopi, and Navajo) had agreed to the placement of the monument on their land and were now participating in the dedication ceremonies. In addition to the children performing in the program, many more Indian children came in by bus to witness this peacemaking event.

In 1942, the Indians were hardly aware of the Japanese. Their resentment was directed against the fork-tongued white man who had killed their ancestors and stolen their land. The Japanese knew little of the Indians, although they brought along some prejudices toward them. As with most of us, they considered other cultures inferior to their own.

The monument somewhat resembles a Japanese lantern with a column towering above. On one of the bronze plaques at the base, we could read with pride and sorrow the names of the 24 Poston *nisei* killed in action in World War II. Around the monument 15 recently-planted palm trees had not yet settled in, so the whole effect remained rather stark.

The pomp and circumstance of the ceremony brought gaiety, sound, and color. The Parker High School Band started up with a rousing march. Then came the insistent beat of the *taiko* drums. In the quiet that followed, a group of Mohave performed a graceful bird dance. The Honor Guard Detachment from Ft. Huachuca posted and later retrieved the colors. Such an American ceremony! The Pledge of Allegiance, an invocation, Sachiye Sugita's "America the Beautiful" solo. The welcoming speeches and words of thanks were all gracious and appropriate. Finally, the surrounding desert reverberated with a 21-gun salute, followed by the ever-poignant taps.

Through it all, I was struck by the coming together of groups so widely divided 50 years earlier:

- The town of Parker, so antagonistic to the "Japs" then, was now represented on a hot Saturday by the high school band;
- The Army had sent a detachment from what had been a segregated Negro training base during the war;
- The Tribal Council of four Native American groups;
- 2,000 Poston evacuees.

The monument towered 38 feet high above the green fields, in seeming affirmation of the words of peace and amity spoken below.

After the dedication program ended, all the visitors were bused over to the La Paz fairground for a barbecue, hosted by the Tribal Council. Faced with hundreds of hot and hungry guests, the hosts somehow fed us generously. Between luscious bites, we talked and remembered, laughed, and sighed.

As Daniel Eddy, Jr., chairman of the Tribal Council, said in his concluding remarks, "May this monument stand as a reminder of an act that should never happen again."

Heartfelt Thanks

Beyond the infinite patience of Arthur Harris, whose forbearance goes back to 1942, I am, currently, most beholden to Debra Castro, who not only designed an inspiring cover, but kept me going for eleven long months; and to Sheila Gardiner, who shared the drudgery of endless revision and proofreading.

To others, also, my debt is huge and unpayable. In the list below, an asterisk indicates exceptional merit and two asterisks indicate extraordinary valor. If I have missed anyone, I sincerely regret the oversight.

Marydel Balderston
* Rich Budnick
Katherine Collins
* Helen Craig
* Barbara Washler Curry
Edward and Edwina Devereux
*** Noriko Sawada Bridges Flynn
* Jane Gubelin
* Jean Guthrie
David and Robert Harris
Bennett Hymer
Sunao Imoto
Frank Iritani
** Sheila James
Miwa Kai
Betsy Kubota
* Elsa Kudo
* Kaye Masatani
* Margaret Masuoka
Dallas and Shiori Kajikawa
McLaren

* John Michimoto
* Nancy Mower
Dennis Ogawa
* Margaret Pai
James Paulauskas
* Frances Cushman Pierce
Harriet Powell
Jane Pultz
Sarah Rice
* Shirley Sanders
** Ben Sanematsu
** Robert J. Smith
* Jane Strong
* Grace Uno
Joyce Wiese
Waimea Willliams
Ella Wiswell
Eddie Yamasaki
James and Marion Yamashita

Each of you knows how helpful you have been in so many different ways. My gratitude is beyond my ability to express. Thank you, one and all.

Finally, thanks to the National Archives for their extensive photographic resources.

Grodzins, Morton. *Americans Betrayed: Politics and the Japanese Evacuation.* University of Chicago Press, 1949.

A devastating account of the pressure groups responsible for making mass evacuation happen and the sins of omission at the federal level.

Hosokawa, Bill. *Nisei: The Quiet Americans.* New York: William Morrow and Company, 1969.

One of the earliest definitive reports on the background history and experience of relocation, along with events that followed the war. A factual, but basically passionate, account of the unfairness of relocation.

Houston, Jeanne Wakatsuki, and James D. Houston. *Farewell to Manzanar.* San Francisco Book Company/Houghton Mifflin edition, 1973; Bantam Books, 1974.

A poignant personal account of a young woman's experience with the bitterness of relocation and her acceptance of it.

Okada, John. *No-No Boy.* Combined Asian American Resources Project, Inc., 1976.

Originally published in 1957, this unheralded novel was an early exploration of what it means to be both American and Japanese, or neither.

Sone, Monica (Otoi). *Nisei Daughter.* Little Brown & Company, 1979. (Copyright 1953).

A wonderfully good-tempered personal account of life up to and through relocation, ending with an acceptance of herself as a Japanese American.

Spicer, Edward H., Asael T. Hansen, Katherine Luomala, and Marvin K. Opler. *Impounded People: Japanese Americans in the Relocation Centers.* University of Arizona Press, 1969.

An even-handed and humane report of the personal conditions and conflicts of evacuees and of staff members in Japanese Relocation

Centers during the years 1942–45, by four anthropologists who were in the Community Analysis Section of the War Relocation Authority.

Uchida, Yoshiko. *Desert Exile: The Uprooting of a Japanese American Family.* University of Washington Press, 1982.

A poignant personal account of one family's uprooting and internment during World War II. An eloquent statement of what it was like to be a Japanese-American before and during the war.

U.S. Commission on Wartime Relocation and Internment of Civilians— *Personal Justice Denied.* Superintendent of Documents, Government Printing Office, 1983.

This government report is based on 750 interviews and a review of materials from government and university archives, and of historical writings. The findings of the Commission finally made redress and reparations possible in 1988.

Weglyn, Michi. *Years of Infamy: The Untold Story of America's Concentration Camps.* New York: Wm. Morrow & Co., Inc., 1976.

A detailed account of background factors leading up to evacuation, description of camps in general with emphasis on Tule Lake, including some information about Canada and Peru. Covers the area of law cases and property settlement after World War II.

There are many, many more books and articles available for the interested reader and much valuable information to be found on websites.

Above: A sketch of the author by an unknown ninth grade student who tucked it into the teacher's class book.